FUN IN JAMAICA

New titles in the series

Barbados

also available

Acapulco
Bahamas
Las Vegas
London
Maui
Montreal
New Orleans
New York City
Paris
Rio
St. Martin/St. Maarten
San Francisco
Waikiki
Walt Disney World and
  the Orlando Area

FUN IN
JAMAICA

Gary Diedrichs

FODOR'S TRAVEL PUBLICATIONS, INC.
New York & London

Contents

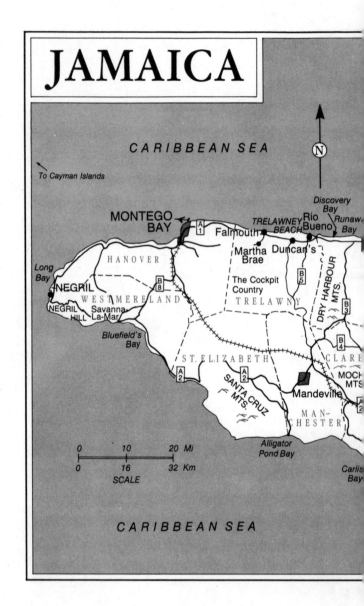

JAMAICA

CARIBBEAN SEA

To Cayman Islands

MONTEGO BAY

Discovery Bay

TRELAWNEY BEACH

Rio Bueno

Runaw Bay

A1 Falmouth

Duncan's

Long Bay

HANOVER

Martha Brae

NEGRIL

The Cockpit Country

B5

DRY HARBOUR MTS.

B8

NEGRIL HILL

WESTMERELAND

Savanna-La-Mar

TRELAWNY

B3

Bluefield's Bay

ST. ELIZABETH

B4

CLARE

A2

A2

SANTA CRUZ MTS.

Mandeville

MOCH MTS

MAN-CHESTER

A2

Alligator Pond Bay

Carlis Bay

0   10   20 Mi
0   16   32 Km
SCALE

CARIBBEAN SEA

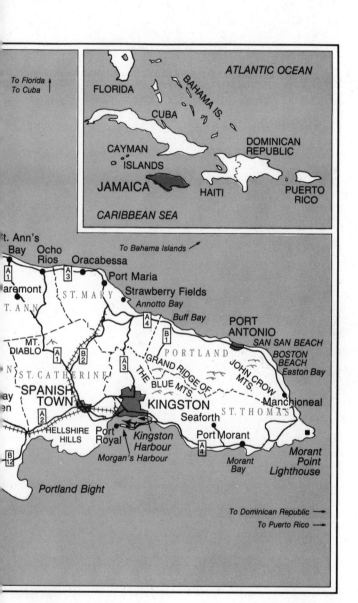

To Florida
To Cuba

ATLANTIC OCEAN

FLORIDA

BAHAMA IS.

CUBA

CAYMAN
ISLANDS

JAMAICA

HAITI

DOMINICAN
REPUBLIC

PUERTO
RICO

CARIBBEAN SEA

t. Ann's
Bay

Ocho
Rios

Oracabessa

To Bahama Islands

aremont

ST. MARY

Port Maria

Strawberry Fields

Annotto Bay

T. ANN

Buff Bay

PORT
ANTONIO

SAN SAN BEACH

MT.
DIABLO

A1

B2

PORTLAND

B1

BOSTON
BEACH

A3

GRAND RIDGE OF

Easton Bay

N

ST. CATHERINE

THE

BLUE MTS.

JOHN CROW
MTS.

SPANISH
TOWN

KINGSTON

ay
en

A2

Seaforth

ST. THOMAS

Manchioneal

HELLSHIRE
HILLS

Port
Royal

Kingston
Harbour

Port Morant

A4

B12

Morgan's Harbour

Morant
Bay

Morant
Point
Lighthouse

Portland Bight

To Dominican Republic →
To Puerto Rico →

Introduction

"No problem, *mon*. . ." Wherever you venture on the island of Jamaica, whatever you ask, the answer is the same. It can be done. Not to worry. Life is to be enjoyed. There is a devotion to *living* here. It is an intense devotion, all-encompassing, and yet no big deal. If you feel like singing, you sing; if you feel like dancing, you dance. No problem, *mon*.

It is difficult, if not impossible, not to join the party. But why resist? The first sight of, say, the young MBA from Chicago, her blond hair newly braided into tight corn rows, swaying to a joyous reggae beat drifting across a splendid expanse of white, powdery sand strikes you as incongruous. You watch as others join in: the lawyer from New York, his T-shirt reading, NO PROBLEM; the honeymooning couple from Atlanta. Soon it's an impromptu celebration.

Off to one side, the tall Jamaican, his dreadlocks tucked into a green-and-black woolen cap is grinning approval and swaying, too. Now you begin to believe that the sweet life in Jamaica really is no problem, *mon*.

Even in a Caribbean dotted with islands of beauty

and magic, there is something special about Jamaica. Its beauty, its magic are expressed in so many different ways.

See them, for example, in the diversity of the Jamaican scenery, one of the richest and most varied in the world . . . From the seven miles of uninterrupted sand along Negril Beach and from those sunny playgrounds of the north shore, Montego Bay and Ocho Rios, to the astonishing eagle's eye views and alpine cool of the Blue Mountains or the high country around the inland town of Mandeville . . . From the low, dark-green, shrimp-filled marshlands edging the Black River to the pock-marked limestone crags of the mysterious Cockpit Country . . . From the capital city of Kingston, chaotic yet mesmerizing, to the calm of the fishing village of Port Antonio.

See them in Jamaica's diverse population. "Out of Many, One People"—so goes the national motto. The nation's 2.3 million citizens are a piquant and pleasing mix of African, European, East Indian, and Chinese. Along the highways, in the villages and towns, your mind can't help but snap unending freeze frames, mental snapshots to summon this time long after you have come and gone: the school children, so fresh in their neatly pressed uniforms, waving, exuberantly as you pass; the weekend cricketers dressed all in white on the long green lawn; the shy young women, gossiping quietly to each other as they tend to the shops behind Kingston's famous Devon House.

And there's 72-year-old Bill Laurie, Scotsman by birth, sitting one fine morning at a small table on the veranda of his hilltop restaurant in Mandeville, sipping rich Jamaican coffee and talking quietly of his grandchildren. Or the woolly-headed man called Prince Julie, displaying his handwoven hammocks by the Negril roadside, who invites you to take a heady whiff of his lima-bean soup that bubbles over an open fire. Or the man "come down from deh mountin" who sells you the heavy walking stick he carved from ironwood. Or the white-gloved waiter named James who chases a peacock out of his path as he delivers a breakfast tray at Trident Villas in Port Antonio.

There's also the music, of course: folk ballads, work songs, revivalist hymns; mento, Jamaica's folk music—

sensuous, irresistible; reggae, influenced by the Rastafarian religious cult, and alive with the memory of Bob Marley and the heartbeat of the people.

The food is colorful and pungent; the drink, ubiquitous rum, Red Stripe beer, as well as nonalcoholic thirst quenchers in exotic flavors like soursop, tamarind, and sorrel.

The flora and fauna? Bougainvillea, hibiscus, oleander, poinsettia, ackee, breadfruit, cassia, guangao, logwood, naseberry, bananas, sugar cane, pimento, coffee. The whistling frog, mongoose, hummingbird, and gloriously plumed doctor bird.

The first human inhabitants, the Arawak Indians, called the island Xaymaca, meaning Land of Wood and Water. It is also a land rich in bauxite—Jamaica is the world's largest producer of this mineral that is smelted into aluminum—as well as limestone, marble, alabaster, and sandstone. In area it is 4,411 square miles, third largest in the Caribbean. At its longest, Jamaica stretches 144 miles; at its widest, 52 miles. From its central backbone of mountains running east to west—the Blue Mountain Peak rises 7,402 feet above the sea—waterfalls, springs, rivers, and streams flow to the fertile plains and beaches which circle the island.

When Christopher Columbus discovered Jamaica in 1494, he called it "the fairest island that eyes have beheld." It was awarded to him and his family by the Spanish government, and the great explorer spent a whole year at New Seville, near St. Ann's Bay. In 1655 the Spanish fled under attack from the British, who retained rule until the independent nation was born in 1962. It remains a member of the British Commonwealth.

This is a country fraught with both promise and poverty. Economic and political problems disrupted the norm in the 1970s; and as recently as 1985 there were disturbances in Kingston following a steep hike in the price of gasoline.

Yet the hope of better days seems more than illusory. The government has worked hard to promote tourism as a primary building block for the future—even to the point of urging its people to smile more. In traditional

Jamaica, a smile is a sign of genuine friendship, some-thing to be earned, rather than a casual form of greeting. At heart, most Jamaicans are old-fashioned and like a show of good manners. When you need assistance, such words as good morning and thanks—"howdy" and "tenky"—will work wonders.

Distances are not great in Jamaica, and most points of interest are accessible on paved roads; yet the novelty of driving on the left, in combination with rutted stret-ches or winding mountain and coastal roads, forces trav-elers to take their time, making a drive of even relatively short distance a mini-adventure.

But by all means make the effort to explore beyond the silky-soft beaches. You'll make serendipitous discov-eries, and you'll find a warm people, justifiably proud of its island home. A sense of curiosity about Jamaica's many marvels is genuinely appreciated. They want you to experience the best.

General Information

The weather in Jamaica? Well, *almost* no problem.
Though a tropical country, Jamaica does have variations
in climate, depending on where you are and the time of
year. From December to April, daytime temperatures
hover between 70 and 80 degrees; in Kingston, though,
the thermometer may well top 90 degrees. Summer read-
ings are usually in the high 80s to low 90s. Trade winds
from the northeast and mountain breezes keep things
pleasant along the coast (by day, the so-called "doctor's
breeze" blows in from the sea, by night the "undertaker's
breeze" blows back to the sea). Year-round, though, the
higher you go, the cooler it gets. Mandeville, perched in
the cool hills of Manchester, as well as the coffee plantations of the Blue Mountains, can be downright refresh-
ing, even crisp—as daytime temperatures dip at least 10
degrees below coastal levels.

   In late spring (May through early June) and autumn
(October to early November), daily rain showers are
common; they're typically brief, cleansing, and followed
by a drying sun. Port Antonio, on the lush northeast
coast, sees the most frequent shower activity, but these,
too, are usually very little problem: the air dampens

under cover of darkness and early morning, but by 11 A.M. another glorious day has begun.

In short, you can be reasonably confident that, apart from the possibility of a few raindrops falling on your head plus their accompanying cloud cover, your stay will not be marred by bad weather. Indeed, perfect beach weather is the most likely forecast. When, then, should you go? If cost and crowds are no impediment, anytime will do. Be advised, however, that mid-December to Easter is peak tourist season—Christmas vacation, especially. Hotel rooms are at their most scarce, prices their highest, and all the tourist attractions their most crowded. Reservations several months in advance are always a good idea. During peak periods, they are virtually essential.

One caveat: Hurricane season begins in June and stretches through October. The likelihood of a direct hit by hurricane is remote, though Hurricane Allen did strike the north coast in 1980.

Phoning Jamaica

The area code for the entire nation of Jamaica is 809; thus, from the United States you simply dial 1–809 and then the local number. If you call after 5 P.M., your local time, rates are surprisingly reasonable and connections often amazingly clear. Be sure to ask that a written confirmation of hotel accommodations be mailed.

When making reservations or inquiries by phone from home, always check first with the "800" information operator (dial 1–800–555–1212) to see if a toll-free number is available for where you're calling. Many of the major Jamaican hotels boast "800" numbers these days.

Within the country, phone service can at times be frustrating; the system is prone to breakdowns and overloads. That, of course, is one more reason to make arrangements for accommodations before arrival.

Emergency numbers for the entire island: Police and Air-Sea Rescue is 119; fire department and ambulance, 110.

JAMAICA TIME

When it's noon in Washington, D.C., it's also noon in the Jamaican capital of Kingston—and all of this island nation. Except in summertime. Jamaican clocks are set on Eastern standard time the year round; daylight-saving time is not observed.

So much for actual time. What about the Jamaican *sense* of time? Expect—and learn to savor—a slower pace, a Caribbean casualness regarding timetables and appointed hours. Things get done, but why rush? "Soon come," as the islanders say. Translation: relax and enjoy.

THE YEAR IN JAMAICA

Banks and most stores are closed on New Year's Day—as they are on Ash Wednesday, Good Friday, Easter Monday, Labour Day (May 23), National Heroes Day (third Monday in October), Christmas, and Boxing Day (December 26).

Toward the end of January, a chance to witness first-class polo is yours at the annual Chukka Cove Cup competition in Ocho Rios (the Caribbean Cup is up for grabs here in late February).

Early March sees Manchester Golf Week in Mandeville, the island's oldest golf tournament, with more than a half-century of tradition behind it. A few weeks later the Miami-to-Montego Bay Yacht Race, begun in 1961, brings excitement and a round of social events. The largest flower show in the Caribbean, well over an acre of flora, is hosted by the Jamaica Horticultural Society in Kingston toward the end of April.

If you're in Kingston in early May, the manicured lawns of King's House—official residence of Jamaica's Governor General—are the site of Her Excellency's May Day Charities, a popular yearly event that includes food, music, and dance. Later in the month, Ocho Rios hosts the Jamaica International Marlin Tournament and the Trelawny Carnival livens up the town of Falmouth with a parade and well-known Caribbean musicians in concert.

August is a month for parades, music, costume pageants, and all the pomp that goes into celebration of the anniversary of Jamaica's birth as a sovereign nation on August 6th, 1962. Partying is most intense in the capital of Kingston, but the whole country joins in. Near month's end Montego Bay is overrun by the thousands who gather from the world over for the five days of the internationally acclaimed Reggae Sunsplash concerts. Around this same time, in Kingston, the Jamaican entry to the annual Miss World contest is crowned at a gala pageant.

A charity event of special note is the Henry Morgan Buccaneer Ball in early October, held in the famous privateer's erstwhile headquarters of Port Royal, near Kingston. Guests don pirate garb—what else? About a week thereafter it's time for one of the oldest and most prestigious sport-fishing contests in the Caribbean, the Port Antonio International Marlin Tournament.

The year rounds out with two of Jamaica's great loves, the show horse and golf. At the beginning of November, in Annotto Bay, the Jamaica Horse Association holds its annual International Horse Trials, two days of dressage, show jumping, and cross-country featuring teams from the U.S., Great Britain, and the host country. Around the third week of November, the Jamaica Open Golf Tournament draws to Kingston professionals and amateurs from round the world. Then, in mid-December, two dozen top golfers from the LPGA and PGA Senior Tour play for what has traditionally been the world's largest purse (a half-million U.S. dollars) for a single tournament. The place: Tryall Golf and Beach Club, Montego Bay.

INFORMATION, PLEASE

The single best source of information and assistance on the island is the Jamaica Tourist Board. Don't hesitate to contact one of the JTB offices before or during your stay.

In the United States: 866 Second Avenue, 10th Floor, New York, NY 10017, 212–688–7650; 36 South Wabash Avenue, Suite 1210, Chicago, IL 60603, 312–346–1546; 3440 Wilshire Boulevard, Suite 1207, Los Angeles, CA 90010, 213–384–1123.

In Jamaica, the JTB is headquartered at 21 Dominica Drive, New Kingston, 929–9200 (mailing address: Tourism Centre Building, New Kingston, Box 360, Kingston 5, Jamaica, W.I.). There are regional offices in Montego Bay (at Cornwall Beach, 952–4425), Ocho Rios (in the Ocean Village Shopping Centre, 974–2570), Port Antonio (at City Centre Plaza, 993–3051), and Negril (at Plaza de Negril, 957–4243).

Tourist board information desks are also staffed at the Montego Bay and Kingston airports.

The best island newspaper is the *Daily Gleaner,* though the *Star* is more lively; both provide useful updates on shopping, dining, nightlife, and special events. An especially good locally published guidebook is Margaret Morris's *Tour Jamaica,* available at many hotels and other tourist venues.

EXTRA ''IRIE''

In the local patois, *irie* means the best imaginable. And if you're looking for a Jamaica beyond the simply great, the "dine-around, stay-over" package known as **Elegant Resorts of Jamaica** may be for you. Under this plan, guests check into one of six ultraluxury resorts— Tryall Golf and Beach Club, Round Hill, or Half Moon Club in Montego Bay; Plantation Inn or the San Souci

Hotel and Club in Ocho Rios; or Trident Villas and Hotel in Port Antonio. Then, for no additional charge, they may dine at any of the other five. For information call 800–237–3237.

Why not rent your own villa, complete with housekeeper (who can usually double as a nanny), gardener, and cook? Jamaica offers villas that run the gamut from quaint and cozy to palatial; from in-town to secluded seaside spots with private tennis courts, swimming pools, and even isolated stretches of beach. Listings of villa representatives are available through the Jamaica Tourist Board. Easier yet, phone the **Jamaica Association of Villas and Apartments** (JAVA) at 800–221–8830; this organization lists nearly 300 rental properties ranging from $750 to more than $4,000 per week.

A final "800" trouble-saver: More than two dozen small and mid-size hostelries across the island, all of reputable quality and most modestly priced, have banded together as the **Inns of Jamaica.** Call for information and reservations at 800–526–2422.

WHAT TO TAKE

Packing shouldn't be a chore, since basic resortwear —shorts, slacks, sport shirts—will serve as the mainstay of your wardrobe. But your destination in Jamaica makes a difference. In Negril, where women can go topless at most beaches and clothing is optional for both sexes at others, casual is the operative word year-round. Yet even in Negril—as throughout the island—short shorts and bathing suits are not considered proper attire for shopping or dining in town, and in the evenings most women switch to pants or skirts.

And even vegetating on the beach means bringing along some cover-ups—long-sleeved shirt, pants, hat or sun visor. Base tan or not, don't forget sunscreen. If taken lightly, the Caribbean sun is *not* forgiving.

In the tonier resorts of Montego Bay, Ocho Rios, and Port Antonio, men are required to wear a jacket (and tie, except in summer) at cocktails and dinner. For the same reason, women should pack at least one lightweight "dress-up" outfit. And in Kingston, the island's governmental and business center, you may feel out of place altogether in shorts, even in the noonday sun. Most Jamaican men in the capital wear long-sleeved shirts and trousers; the women, modestly cut dresses.

Up the cooler mountains a sweater or light jacket will certainly come in handy.

Take the absolute minimum. Airlines restrict the number and weight of bags you may bring—Air Jamaica, for instance, limits coach passengers to two bags apiece weighing not more than 44 pounds. Save room to bring home that hand-carved ironwood walking stick or hand-made hammock. The shops are also full of wonderfully colorful beach- and casual-wear.

Don't forget sunglasses and an appropriate beach read—say, Peter Matthiessen's *Far Tortuga,* a highly original novel set in the Caribbean. Film is expensive on the island, so if you pack a camera, bring all you'll need. Ditto cigarettes and drug-store items. It's worth hauling along a small first-aid kit, plus remedies for headache and upset stomach, just in case. If you're traveling with a small child, disposable diapers, formula, and baby food are easily found in the main tourist areas—though, again, at higher prices than back home.

GETTING THERE

By air Jamaica lies only three-and-a-half hours from New York, less than 90 minutes from Miami, about five hours from either Dallas or Los Angeles. For 12 weeks in the winter of 1987, though, Montego Bay was but an hour and 45 minutes from New York's John F. Kennedy Airport—as Air Jamaica, the island's national carrier, inaugurated weekly Concorde service, a first in the Caribbean.

Whether the Concorde—which cruises at 1,340 m.p.h., literally faster than a speeding bullet—renews its

New York-to-Jamaica connection in future high tourist seasons will depend on the success of its maiden flights. But year-round Air Jamaica flies its regular aircraft to both Montego Bay and Kingston from Atlanta, Baltimore, Los Angeles, Miami, New York, Philadelphia, Tampa, and Toronto. Other carriers flying to both island destinations: Air Canada from Toronto; American from New York and Boston; BWIA from San Juan; and Eastern from Miami.

To Montego Bay only, Eastern flies from Atlanta and Air Canada from Montreal. Montego Bay's Donald Sangster International Airport is most convenient to Negril, Ocho Rios, and coastal points between, while Kingston's Norman Manley Airport is best for Port Antonio and Mandeville. Trans Jamaican Airlines runs air shuttles linking Kingston, Mandeville, Montego Bay, Negril, Ocho Rios, and Port Antonio.

Check with the airline or your travel agent for the latest on fares and their requirements. And remember that, before your return, the airline requires reconfirmation of your reservation at least 72 hours prior to departure. Should you forget, your seat might be resold.

You might also care to investigate a money-saving package that combines air fare with a hotel room and other extras such as rental car, entertainment, and dining discounts. It's not uncommon that the total cost of such a package—eight days at a good beachfront hotel, say, plus roundtrip airfare and more—can be had for what you would ordinarily pay for airfare alone.

Of course, Jamaica is also a popular stopover for cruise ships plying the Caribbean. Most of these leave from Miami, Tampa, or Port Everglades, and their ports of call include Montego Bay, Ocho Rios, Port Antonio, and Kingston.

WHEN YOU ARRIVE

Upon arrival, you face the island's immigration and customs officials. For U.S. and Canadian citizens a passport (it can be up to a year beyond its expiration date) is identification enough but is not required; in its place *two* of the following may be presented: residency card or certificate (for legal residents who are not U.S. or Canadian citizens), naturalization certificate or card, driver's license with photo, voter's registration card, or birth certificate. Married women using birth certificates should also bring a copy of their marriage licenses.

Customs allows personal items duty free (though on the flight you will be asked to declare everything on a customs form). Not allowed are rum, pets, raw meats, flowers, and firearms.

There are no vaccination or other health requirements for entry (unless you are arriving from a country where serious contagion exists), nor do you need to take any special medical precautions. Even the water is safe to drink.

WHEN YOU LEAVE FOR HOME

Again, remember to reconfirm your airline reservation at least 72 hours in advance of your flight. And be sure to save enough Jamaican currency to pay the departure tax of J\$40 per person.

As you scout the airport for ways to spend other remaining island currency, keep the following in mind:

Jamaican Blue Mountain Coffee. The price for this world-renowned brew—whole beans or ground—is virtually the same throughout the country, even in the Blue Mountains. Roughly, it will cost about half what it goes for in most gourmet shops or coffee stores in the States (the exact price, naturally, fluctuates with the exchange rate and market supply). If you intend to buy several pounds—attractively packaged in individual burlap coffee bags and vacuum-sealed foil for freshness—you might as well wait to buy your coffee at the airport just before departing.

Fresh Jamaican flowers. Airport shops have inexpensive preboxed assortments of such beautiful tropical flora as anthurium and poinciana. Tempting as they are, an agricultural inspector will more than likely confiscate them when you land back in the U.S.

Duty-free goods. These can *only* be purchased with credit card, traveler's check, U.S. or Canadian currency. And don't forget that although "duty free" can mean prices as much as half off those charged back home, U.S. Customs *will* levy duty charges if you return with more than the allowable limit of $400, including one liter of alcohol per adult. Duty-free liquor, cigarettes, and Jamaican cigars can only be purchased at the pier or airport.

Money

Money matters can get a bit confusing, since Jamaicans also call their legal tender the dollar. And while new regulations require that Jamaican currency must be used for all cash purchases (except at duty-free shops, as noted above), the Jamaicans themselves, especially in prime tourist areas, sometimes quote prices in U.S. dollars. The difference is substantial: Though the rate of exchange fluctuates, at press time the Jamaican dollar was worth just under 20 cents (U.S.).

Currency can be exchanged at airport bank counters, cruise-ship piers, commercial banks, and in nearly all hotels. The daily rate is the same everywhere on the island, so your hotel is almost always the quickest and best place to buy Jamaican dollars. Most banks are open between 9 A.M. and 2 P.M., Monday through Thursday; Fridays they close at noon, then reopen from 2:30 to 5 P.M.

Make sure to get a receipt. Without one, you won't be able to reconvert Jamaican currency before going home. Only airport and cruise-pier bank counters are authorized to reconvert—and it is illegal to take Jamaican dollars into or out of the country.

Of course, major credit cards and traveler's checks are also widely accepted by hotels, restaurants, and shops.

Note: Unless specifically noted otherwise, all prices quoted in this book are in U.S. dollars and are subject to fluctuations in the exchange rate. Room rates quoted exclude tax and service charge and are given for the high season (from mid-April to mid-December, they drop as much as half).

SPEAKING JAMAICAN

Jamaica's ties to Great Britain go back three centuries, and English is the official language. Among themselves, however, Jamaicans frequently speak a patois that is a rhythmic and lilting mixture of English, African, Creole, and islandisms.

A few examples from the amusing *How to Speak Jamaican* by Ken Maxwell (distributed locally):

"It irie." It's first class, excellent.

"Tandey till me come." Stay there till I come.

"Have you any flim fe de camera?" Is there film in your camera?

GETTING AROUND

Unless you must have one, don't rent a car for your entire stay. They are very expensive—a compact car with air-conditioning for a week, for instance, runs from $375 to $400. Gasoline is equally pricey—about $2 an imperial gallon (one-fifth larger than the U.S. gallon). Although the highways are generally good, they're poorly marked, if at all; and you've got to make the adjustment to driving on the left (this was a British colony, remember?) Finally, should you smash up the rental, most agreements put your liability at the first $400 in damages, or more.

If you still want a car, do reserve it beforehand. Especially in peak season, they are all but impossible to rent once you're on the island. The big chains have toll-free numbers, making reservations easy; ask for a written confirmation and bring it with you.

You won't need an international driver's license. A valid U.S. or Canadian license is sufficient. But unless you are paying by credit card, you will be asked for a cash deposit of several hundred dollars.

Among the dozen or more rental outfits on the island, try: Avid (800–331–2112), Dollar (800–421–6868), Hertz (800–654–3131), National (800–328–4567); or Island (926–8012 in Kingston, 952–5771 in Montego Bay).

A much less expensive and more adventuresome means of personal transport is a moped or motor scooter. These can be rented from most major hotels, or at rental agencies. Stony Hill Castle Ltd. Bike Rentals has locations in Negril (next to the police station, 957–4460), Montego Bay (Holiday Inn Village Shopping Centre, 953–2292), and Ocho Rios (58 Main Street, 974–2681); it charges about $18 a day for a scooter and $38 for either a trail bike or Honda CM200 motorcycle, plus a deposit of about $40 and $100 (a credit-card voucher will do), respectively.

Most visitors, though, find it best to rely on taxis for short hauls. Easy to find at airports and most hotels, they can also be summoned by telephone or hailed at curbside. They charge by the car, not per passenger, and thus can be quite reasonable when three or more share the fare. Taxi drivers also make wonderful tour guides, especially if you ask your hotel to set up a drive with a friendly and knowledgeable cabbie.

Keep in mind: Not all taxis are metered, so come to an understanding on the fare ahead of time. For out-of-the-way destinations, ask the cabbie to return for you at a specified time. From midnight to 5 A.M., a 25 percent surcharge is added to the metered fare or posted rate. All licensed taxis display red PPV (Public Passenger Vehicle) plates.

In Kingston and Montego Bay, buses are frequent and a cheap means of transport. Check with the Jamaican Tourist Board offices for routes, rates, and times. Minibuses also play these routes, but they're often so crowded that passengers literally hang off the sides. Bus trips to other island locations are likely to be an adventure, at best, shared not only with great numbers of Jamaicans, but also with huge amounts of freight and luggage as well as produce and chickens bound for market.

There's yet another alternative: Jamaica Railway runs its diesel trains daily between Kingston and Montego Bay, a remarkable inexpensive, five-hour journey that's sure to be memorable if you're in the mood and have the time to spare. About $5 first class (weekends only), $3 coach. Phone 922–6620 in Kingston; 952–4842 in Montego Bay.

The quickest means to travel between major points on the island is by air. Trans Jamaican Airlines (923–8680 in Kingston; 957–4251 in Negril; 952–5401 in Montego Bay; 974–3254 in Ocho Rios; 993–2791 in Port Antonio) connects Kingston, Montego Bay, Negril, Ocho Rios, and Port Antonio. Book in advance through a travel agent, if possible. The Kingston-to-Port Antonio fare, for instance, is about $40.

A final transportation tip: Try to arrange your airport transfer in advance through a travel agent or when making hotel reservations (if that service is provided). Taxi fares from Montego Bay's Sangster Airport to local hotels will run perhaps $10, but to Ocho Rios it can cost upwards of $60. From Norman Manley Airport in Kingston to Port Antonio, it's as much as $65.

GUIDED TOURS

The tour operators are several, the options many, but well regarded are Estate Tours (974–2058 in Ocho Rios), Greenlight Tours (953–2824 in Montego Bay, 926–1620 in Kingston), Jamaica Tours (952–2887 in Montego Bay), and Martin's Jamaica (926–1351 in Kingston,

962–2203 in Mandeville, 952–4350 in Montego Bay, 974 –2594 in Ocho Rios, 993–2625 in Port Antonio).

Half-day excursions are usually priced at under $10; a full day about $15, not including lunch.

Sights well worth touring with a guide include the Great Houses—Devon House, Greenwood, and Rose Hall—and the plantations—Brimmer Hall and Prospect —as well as Kingston, Montego Bay, and Ocho Rios.

On Wednesdays from Montego Bay, the Hilton High Day Tour (also known as the "Up, Up and Buffet") costs a steep $48 per person, but is certainly the most uplifting tour on the island. After an early-morning motor to a former banana plantation near Negril and a Jamaican breakfast, a tethered hot-air-balloon ride takes you aloft, albeit briefly; there follows a tour of the planta- tion and the German village of Seaford Town, a sumptu- ous suckling-pig luncheon, rum drinks, perhaps a hike or horseback ride. The same tour leaving from Negril costs $55. Reserve through your hotel, or phone 952–3343.

Another popular all-day experience is the Gover- nor's Coach Tour. A railway coach car that once was the private conveyance of Jamaica's governors travels 40 miles into the interior from Montego Bay, with stops at the Appleton Rum Distillery, the Ipswich Caves, a charm- ing riverbank for a picnic lunch, and Catadupa (where you can buy fabric for a dress or sport shirt on the way up and pick up the finished product on the way back). A bar and calypso band are all aboard, too. Tuesday through Friday, the train pulls out of the station at 9:30 A.M. and returns at 5 P.M. A ticket goes for about $32, including lunch and a rum drink. Book as early as possi- ble with Jamaica Tours (952–2887).

Premier Tours (952–5919) hosts a Thursday train journey to the Appleton rum works combined with a bus tour of the town of Mandeville. Two meals plus enter- tainment and rum punch along the way cost about $45 per person.

Meet the People

For two decades now, the Meet the People program has successfully brought together visitors and Jamaicans with similar backgrounds and interests. For a day, or even a few hours, feel like you're no longer a tourist, but a welcome guest. The Meet the People volunteers include teachers, nurses, musicians, sportsmen, artists, journalists, businessmen, and others with enthusiasms ranging from painting to polo to poker.

Together, you might watch a play, go to church, or simply visit with the friends and family of your host.

The idea is to provide an opportunity for a cultural exchange that goes beyond the usual tourist experience, and it works. You might even make a real friend. Best of all, it's free of charge. Simply contact the nearest Jamaica Tourist Board office.

Other tips

● **Drugs.** Chances are, you *will* be approached by street "higglers" peddling the renowned island marijuana—called *ganja*—or cocaine. Just remember that these drugs are illegal. Getting arrested with them in your possession will almost certainly result in a heavy fine and an early trip home.

● **Electric current.** In most hotels, it's 110 volts—just like at home. A few offer both 110 and 220. Those with only 220 usually supply converters or adapters for hair dryers and electric shavers.

● **Postage.** Postcards to North America, via airmail, require postage of 45 cents, Jamaican; letters are 55 cents per half ounce.

● **Religion.** Most Jamaicans are Christians, and all the major denominations have churches on the island. Other small religious congregations are Jews, Hindus, Bahais, and Moslems.

- **Tipping.** Restaurants and hotels add a service charge, and thus no tipping is necessary; it's best to inquire. Otherwise, 10 to 15 percent is fine. At some all-inclusive resorts, no tipping is allowed.

- **Marriage.** Yes, you can get a marriage license after 24 hours' residence, and most hotels will arrange your wedding.

- **Photographs.** Jamaicans do not like to be snapped without permission. Ask first, and you'll almost always get a yes; sometimes a small tip is requested.

- **Safety.** Use ordinary caution, since there is crime even in this paradise. Ignore suggestions that you accompany anyone to out-of-the-way locales, for whatever reason. On the highway, police roadblocks may stop cars and buses for valid licenses, firearms, and illegal drugs. Don't be alarmed and keep calm.

- **Water.** It's filtered and purified and safe to drink anywhere.

The North Coast

This is the Jamaica of legend . . . the island paradise of sugar-soft sand and romantic waterfalls . . . of the Blue Lagoon and reggae till dawn. This is the Jamaica that welcomes the winter-weary and the stressed-out, and dedicates itself to rejuvenation and the perfect tan.

But yet a beach is not a beach is not a beach. The resorts of the North Coast are as distinct in mood and style as are, say, New York and Los Angeles. Here's where to find *your* place in the sun for the perfect vacation you've always dreamed of.

A reminder: Hotel rates are in U.S. currency before tax and service charge; they are subject to fluctuations in the rate of exchange. We quote peak season figures. Prices from mid-April to mid-December can drop by as much as half, so if your budget is a consideration you might think about visiting Jamaica during these off-peak months.

NEGRIL

Everything you've heard about Negril is true. Nestled at the island's westernmost point, it is the do-as-you-please capital of Jamaica. Casual to a fault, it is a barefoot paradise dedicated to whatever floats your boat. A few years back the pleasures of Negril were an open secret to wool-hatted Rastafarians, hedonistic wanderers, adventurous college kids, and those who wanted to sample the island's legendary *ganja* and other illicit substances with the least chance of rude interruption. Clothing was optional on its beaches, and life was sweet, *mon.*

Today, late-model hippies and swinging singles are being joined by an ever-growing number of peace-loving souls of every stripe attracted by Negril's justly renowned luminous white sand, lush greenery, and spectacular sunsets. Here, all manner of peoples, native and tourist, famous and infamous, wealthy and budget-minded, mingle with an ease and affability not found elsewhere.

LODGING

Accommodations in Negril reflect the diversity of its visitors, yet all share one welcome characteristic: A strict code limits the height of buildings to that of the average palm tree. Thus, while you will find no high-rises, your choices can span the gamut from all-inclusive splendor to a thatched-roof cottage.

About four miles north of the village, on the beach at Rutland Point, is the Club Med-like **Hedonism II** (957 –4200), Box 25, Negril. Like several other havens of hedonism on the island, there are only two ground rules here: First, your room rate covers everything except phone calls and personal laundry—including the hotel's host of activities, meals, drinks, cigarettes, even tips. Second, this is a couples resort. If you don't arrive with a roommate, one (of the same sex) will be assigned to your room; and no one under 16 years of age may stay here.

What's to do here? How about lessons in horseback riding, sailing, parasailing, water-skiing, scuba, snorkel, and Jamaican culture? You'll also find six lighted tennis courts, swimming pool with whirlpool, Nautilus equipment, a library, and virtually nonstop fun-and-games activities like bikini-judging contests for both men and women. There are also two nude beaches, including one on Booby Cay (an awkward bird, by the way). When the sun goes down, you've already found one of the swingingest discos on the entire island.

In several two-story buildings, the 250 guests rooms are bright, modern, and recently refurbished; they are air-conditioned and have private baths. All this, for about $990 a week per person.

Just south along this strand of gorgeous beach, nearly hidden in the coconut palms, lies **Sandals II** (957–4254; toll-free 800–327–1991). More intimate than its rollicking neighbor, this resort is no less comprehensive. Formerly the Coconut Cove, it has received a complete revamping under the new ownership, which runs the highly successful, original Sandals in Montego Bay. All water sports, tennis, meals, drinks, and much more are included at this gem with 32 apartment-style guest rooms. The weekly package runs in the vicinity of $2,300 per couple.

The Sundowner (957–4225), Box 5, Negril, is a small and casual beachfront hotel known for its long-standing dedication to the simple pleasures of sun worship and water sports. Hearty Jamaican fare is served in the dining room near water's edge—the Wednesday buffet and Sunday barbecue are locally famous and a band livens things up on some nights. If it's too quiet, you can always hike the short distance up the beach to Hedonism II. But quiet does not mean boring. Artist Norman Rockwell used to find inspiration here as often as possible.

The 26 rooms are air-conditioned, have two double or king-sized beds, patio or porch. Doubles are about $155 per night.

A bit further south along Norman Manley Boulevard, also known as Route A1—the road that traces the Seven Mile Beach—a newer and welcome destination is the **Negril Gardens** (957–4408; toll-free 800–243–9420), Negril P.O., Negril. Managing Director John Sinclair opened the first phase of his pink-and-white hostelry on quiet, manicured grounds across the road from the beach in spring 1986, including a charming open-air bar and restaurant; and another bar and terrace overlooking a spacious pool and tennis courts.

A little more than a year later, the hotel expanded onto a two-and-a-half-acre beach site, adding another bar and restaurants, shops, and 40 additional guest rooms to the original 16 across the road.

All the rooms have colonial-style porches—where breakfast can be taken—and are air-conditioned, with pitched wooden ceilings, carpeting, French windows, king or double beds, and satellite TV. The staff is helpful and efficient. The double-occupancy rate is $80 per night.

Further south on Norman Manley Boulevard, watch for **T-Water Cottages** (957–4270), Box 11, Negril. This establishment is noteworthy in at least two ways—for its paradisiacal setting on Long Bay Beach and for its colorful owner, Desmond Segree, a local character par excellence. Water sports are the thing here—boating, windsurfing, deep-sea fishing, parasailing, snorkeling, scuba diving, and water-skiing can all be arranged. There's also an informal Jamaican-fare restaurant, beach bar, and nighttime disco.

The 60 air-conditioned units all have private baths. They start at around $75; beachfront suites are $150.

Still a few minutes' drive from the roundabout that marks "downtown" Negril—and easy to miss from the highway—is the cozy and serene **Charela Inn** (957–4277), Box 33, Negril. The Spanish-style inn, housing a dining room that serves affordable Jamaican and French cuisine and a small bar, is steps away from the talc-smooth sand and the sea. The Grizzles, who oversee this user-friendly destination, know most everything there is to know about Negril, and can set you up in anything from a Sunfish to a yacht.

The best rooms are the pair over the dining room and the honeymoon suite up the spiral staircase; the others—there are only 10 in all—string away from the beach and do not have sea views. They are air-conditioned and have private baths. Rates start at $100 per night for two; the honeymoon suite is $110.

Continuing along the coast past the village, on the road that ends at the Negril lighthouse, there rises from the sea rugged cliffs topped by open-air bars, restaurants, souvenir sellers—and more rustic accommodations. Really want to get away from it all, island-style? Then follow the ribbon of roadway up these cliffs until, on the sea side, you spot the **Rock House** (no phone; in the U.S. call 312–296–1894). There's no beach here, but you can plunge into ultramarine pools and coves from your rocky perch; the snorkeling or scuba diving is fine. Or be content simply to listen to the sea lap against the coast while you dive into a good read.

Be assured you'll have a tale to tell back at school or at the office. Your home away from home will be one of half a dozen thatched rondavels—round wooden cottages that seem to have sprouted up from the earth. Oh, yes . . . no phones, no electricity. Your back-to-nature lair is lighted by kerosene lamp. Some of the cottages—which rent in the $50 to $80 range—have kitchenettes, but Rick's Cafe and other dining options are a short walk away.

EXPLORING

Those who seek out Negril solely to eat, drink, and be slothful are doubly blessed. Not only is this an ideal setting in which to perfect the art of all three, there's little reason to do anything else. You'll risk no guilt trip by skipping the local museums and architectural marvels. There are no local museums or architectural marvels.

The historically minded might note that the resort Hedonism II faces what is now called Negril harbor, but is better known as **Bloody Bay**—so named because whalers used to clean their catch here. It was also here that "Calico Jack" Rackham and his female partners in piracy, Anne Bonney and Mary Read, were caught in 1720.

Those who feel the need of excursion should consider these alternatives: Montego Bay is 47 miles distant along the coast-hugging Route A1. To the southeast, Savanna-la-Mar ("the plain by the sea"), a sugar port founded in 1703, is only 19 miles away. Its still-bustling wharf is near the end of Great George Street, the longest city street on the island, and next to the stone remains of the Old Fort (converted into a public swimming pool).

From here, by all means push on another 32 miles to **Black River,** with its many Georgian-style buildings; less than half-way there, on the grounds of Bluefields House near the Bluefields police station, is a breadfruit tree said by some to have been planted by the famous Captain Bligh in the 1790s.

Ten miles beyond Black River Route A2 brings you to Bamboo Avenue, a three-mile stretch of road between Holland Estate and Lacovia that is one of the most-photographed spots in Jamaica. Bamboos planted in the 19th century arch across the road from both sides, forming a living cathedral ceiling. Nearing this memorable sight, you pass through the Great Morass, a freshwater swamp that is also a crocodile refuge. Women vendors at the roadside will entice you with packages of plump, pink shrimp; they're delicious but not for the meek—they're peppery.

A more demanding trip takes you inland to Seaford Town, where many residents are descendants of early 19th-century German settlers; and to the edge of the mysterious Cockpit Country, much of which is still unexplored. The best route is to follow Route A2 past Savanna-la-Mar to Ferris Cross, then head north on Route B8 until the town of Whithorn; there, take the road that heads east through Darliston, Woodstock, Struie, and Rat Trap into Seaford Town. Figure two hours' driving time each way, at least, much of it on road surfaces of dubious quality.

There's an easier way to make this last excursion—and in addition to round-trip transportation it also includes breakfast, a tethered hot-air balloon ride, tour of a former banana plantation and Seaford Town, and a roasted suckling-pig luncheon. It's called "Up, Up and Buffet," costs about $55 per person, and leaves at 6:30 A.M. from Negril on Wednesdays. Contact the Jamaica

Tourist Board office in Negril (957–4243) or Hilton High, the tour operator, in Montego Bay (952–3343).

Montego Bay

MoBay. Christopher Columbus called it "the gulf of good weather." It was once a prime exporter of sugar and bananas. Today it thrives because it is Jamaica's prime arrival port for a major import—you the visitor. Jamaica's second largest city (population 43,500), Montego Bay exists almost wholly to serve the annual invasion of vacationers.

Jets stream in from cold northern cities, giving visitors an awe-inspiring aerial view of a gently undulating landscape dotted with velvety golf courses, swimming pools of all shapes and sizes, and winding streets, surrounded by a calm, clear sea that is a patchwork of blues and greens. Cruise ships glide past Doctor's Cave Beach, one of the island's best, and the bustle of the bay. No matter how you arrive, you'll find a place that can be both calming and confusing. But the more you know of its special places, the more you'll be seduced by MoBay and its multitude of charms.

Lodging

Nowhere else in the Caribbean is there a greater choice in type and style of accommodations. Head east from Donald Sangster International Airport (take Route A1, the Queen's Drive, until it intersects Kent Avenue, turn left), and you are only minutes away from **Sandals** (952–5510; toll-free 800–327–1991), Box 100, Montego Bay. And at this all-inclusive beach resort, you and your significant other (Sandals "fits pairs") can partake of all or none of the host of activities. Food and drink, scuba and other water sports and lessons, constant games and contests, theme parties, plus use of the tennis courts, squash court, health club, pool, sauna, and Jacuzzi—it's all included in one package price for seven-night stays (three-nighters are available in off-peak months).

Package rates for the 173 air-conditioned rooms start at about $1,925 a week per couple and go as high as $2,500 a week for one-bedroom, beachfront villa suites.

Four miles east of the airport on Route A1, in an attractive arc around lush gardens and overlooking Mahoe Bay, is the **Royal Caribbean** (953–2231), Box 167, Montego Bay. Recently transformed into another "all-inclusive," this resort offers both a private beach (water sports galore) and a lovely free-form pool, three tennis courts (two are lighted), and a putting green. A dozen Jamaican colonial buildings contain 165 comfortable guest rooms, with weekly rates, all meals and drinks included, varying from $900 to $1,150 per person.

More traditional accommodations can be had a few miles further east, at **Holiday Inn Rose Hall** (953–2485; toll-free 800–465–4329), Box 480, Montego Bay. Its on-the-beach site, plus the recent complete overhaul of this high-rise by the Holiday Inn chain, make it a good choice for those who seek a familiar middle-of-the-road hostelry. The usual water-sports activities, a pool and private beach, decent food at the hotel restaurant, an arcade of shops, and popular nighttime entertainments also recommend it. Its 520 rooms are air-conditioned and start at around $110 for a double.

Next to the Holiday Inn but truly a world apart is the **Half Moon Club** (953–2211), Box 80, Montego Bay. It is vast—some 400 acres, with the feel of an exclusive country club. It is deluxe—some villa suites have private pools. And since 1955 it has provided about as much luxury and as many top-shelf diversions as any resort in the Caribbean. The spectacular 18-hole Robert Trent Jones golf course has a club house that becomes a fine dining room in the evenings. On the mile-long private beach, a full spectrum of water sports is available; or you may stick with one of the seldom-busy freshwater pools. There are four night-lighted squash courts, 13 tennis courts (pro on duty, four lighted), and a health spa; horseback riding can be arranged.

The Sunday buffet lunch is special, as are bonfire barbecues on the beach.

General Manager Heinz Simonitsch has presided over a recent $6 million expansion and renovation of this property, which includes a striking new dining and bar area and new suites done by noted island architect Earl Levy. There are 197 suites and apartments in all, and these range from $190 to $340 for a one-bedroom villa with maid and cook. Also, for those who favor the all-inclusive approach, the four-day, three-night "Platinum Plan" provides a room plus all meals, drinks, sports, and airport transfers for $1,500 per couple.

Another first-rate choice is the **Wyndham Rose Hall Beach and Country Club** (953–2650; toll-free 800–822–4200), Box 999, Montego Bay. About nine miles east of the airport, this is another island property that has been upgraded and is now managed by the Dallas-based hotel chain. The beachfront location, as you would expect, means that all manner of water sports are but steps from your room; there's also a good-sized pool, an 18-hole championship golf course, and a half-dozen tennis courts with a pro for lessons. Dining possibilities include the Great House Verandah, in the main high-rise hotel, or the country club; the Junkanoo disco is fun for late-night dancing.

In all, 500 well-appointed, air-conditioned rooms, each with private balcony, are housed in twin seven-story towers. They range from $120 to $140 for a double.

Other lodging choices await toward downtown. (From the airport, take Route A1, the Queen's Drive, until it forks into Sunset Avenue, which ends at Kent Avenue, the hotel action strip along the waterfront.) The **Toby Inn** (952–4370), 1 Kent Avenue, is perfect for the budget-minded. An intimate, casual in-town hostelry set amid gardens, it has a pool, a Chinese-Polynesian restaurant, and a coffee shop. Both Cornwall and Doctor's Cave beaches are a short walk away. Many places to eat, shop, and play are within easy hiking distance. All rooms have private bath; some are air-conditioned, some have paddle fans. They go for as little as $65 a night for a double.

Practically across the street (but officially on Gloucester Avenue) is **Jack Tar Village** (952–4340), Box

362, Montego Bay. This is another all-inclusive hotel—at a somewhat lower tariff than most others of its ilk. The location is convenient—it's on the water, with shopping and downtown MoBay nearby. Most of the 128 rooms have a sea view; all are air-conditioned and have private bath. Unlike most all-inclusives, families with children are accepted here. A rate of $160 single, $260 double pays the whole freight, including meals and extras.

Just north on Kent Avenue is another good value. The **Carlyle Beach** (952–4140; reservations at 305–271–0045), Box 412, Montego Bay, is on the inland side of the road, but there's nearby beach access and a pool on the premises. This is a cheery, friendly place with a much-frequented pub and dining room; often there is entertainment in the evening. Fifty-two balconied rooms afford sea views; all have air-conditioning and private bath. About $100 a night for two.

Casa Montego (952–4150), 2 Kent Avenue, is a nine-story affair with a Mediterranean flavor. It's on the inland side of the road, but Doctor's Cave Beach is an easy jaunt. Its impressive saltwater pool is usually busy. There's a dining room, open-air bar, shopping arcade, and disco as well. The 129 air-conditioned rooms have private baths and terraces. This is also an all-inclusive resort—$220 a day per person includes all meals, drinks, and water sports.

Next door is the more moderately priced **Doctor's Cave Beach Hotel** (952–4355), Box 94, Montego Bay. Although not on the beach, this is a comfortable and convenient place, and the glorious sand is a short walk away. Pool, pleasant terrrace restaurant, frequent entertainment. These 79 air-conditioned rooms, all with private bath, go for about $80 double.

Perched 500 feet above sea level, on a quiet hillside above town, the **Richmond Hill Inn** (952–3859) is an 18th-century great house that affords an exemplary view of MoBay itself as well as of the surrounding tropical coastline. The hotel is justly famed for its romantic terrace restaurant, which serves some of the best Jamaican cuisine in the area, and its busy bar. The beach is a few minutes' car or taxi ride away, but there's a pool. The 23 guest rooms are modern, air-conditioned, and have private baths. A double room costs about $90 a night.

Ten miles west of town along the coastal Route A1, on a lush and green peninsula, is a classically elegant enclave that enjoys an international reputation. **Round Hill** (952–5150), Box 64, Montego Bay, is set on 98 garden acres. Most of the accommodations here are privately owned villas, several with private pools, all with loyal staff, available for rent in the owners' absence. There's an exquisite private beach where every variety of water sport is pursued by day, lavish barbecues by night. Tennis can be enjoyed on the grounds; golf privileges are extended at nearby Tryall Golf and Beach Club.

Dinner and dancing (jacket and tie, or black tie, on Saturdays) in the rambling Pineapple House, the main building, is often followed by a nightcap in the bar huddled around the same piano played by Noel Coward, Cole Porter, Irving Berlin, and Leonard Bernstein. We're talking *Lifestyles of the Rich and Famous* here.

The 100 units include 36 guest rooms in Pineapple House (available in winter only); no children or singles in February. Villa suites range from about $300 to $400 a night, breakfast and dinner included; the hotel rooms, closer to the sea, are $280, also with two meals a day.

A dozen miles west of town lies another oasis. The centerpiece of **Tryall Golf and Beach Club** (952–5110; toll-free 800–336–4571) is historic Tryall Great House, built on a hilltop in 1834. As the resort name indicates, golf is the game here. The 18-hole course is best on the island, and annually plays host to the PGA; it's also one of the most beautiful, with stunning seaside views. And the beach part? It's a lovely crescent—recently improved —where water sports can be enjoyed with abandon. The Beach Cafe in the clubhouse is perfect for a casual water's edge lunch, and the great house has a dining room noted for its international cuisine and evening entertainment on the terrace. And there's a swim-up bar at the main pool.

Main pool? Yes, secluded among the trees and gardens of Tryall's rolling 2,200 acres are 40 villas, each with its own swimming hole. Plus a cook, chambermaid, laundress, and gardener. As at Round Hill, the villas are privately owned but can be rented. Two-bedrooms go for $3,000 a week; three-bedrooms are $4,000; four-bedrooms are $5,000. In the great house another 44 distinctive guest rooms range from $260 to $310 a night, including breakfast and dinner.

EXPLORING

Echoes of Montego Bay's past are faint, but resonant. Shortly before Queen's Drive ends at the roundabout, a trio of cannons pointing seaward signal the remains of 16th-century **Fort Montego.** Continuing south onto St. James Street, the main drag through town, brings you to **Sam Sharpe Square** (formerly Charles Square and The Parade). The intriguing little structure in the square's northwest corner is The Cage.

The Cage was erected in 1806 as a jail for slaves and runaway seamen, and today it houses a small museum of pre- and postslave era artifacts and artwork. It's open 10 A.M. to 6 P.M. daily.

A few blocks east, at Union and East Streets, a crumbling stone amphitheater is another remnant of the slave trade. Known as **The Slave Ring,** it is said to have been the town slave market.

Southeast of the square, at Church and St. Claver, limestone **St. James Parish Church** is set in a lovely tropical garden and is itself an admirable restoration (after a 1957 earthquake) of a handsome 1775 Georgian structure. Check out the elegant monuments inside.

West of the square lies Harbour Street, abustle with fishermen unloading their catch and burly stevedores handling fruit, produce, and other local goods for shipment. The **Crafts Market** is here also. To experience a market the way Jamaicans themselves do, try the **Fustic Street market.** Continue south from the square to Barnett Street; Fustic intersects less than a half mile further, on the right. Especially on a Friday or Saturday, the place is a carnival of sights, sounds, and smells. Come prepared to bargain with the women higglers who run the show.

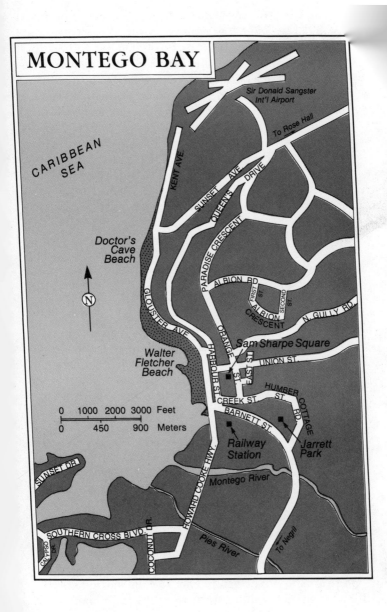

MONTEGO BAY

CARIBBEAN SEA

Sir Donald Sangster Int'l Airport

To Rose Hall

KENT AVE.

SUNSET AVE.

QUEEN'S DRIVE

PARADISE CRESCENT

Doctor's Cave Beach

N

ALBION RD.

FIRST ST.

SECOND ST.

ALBION CRESCENT

N. GULLY RD.

GLOUSTER AVE.

Sam Sharpe Square

Walter Fletcher Beach

HARBOUR ST.

ORANGE ST.

EAST ST.

UNION ST.

HUMBER ST.

COTTAGE RD.

CREEK ST.

BARNETT ST.

| 0 | 1000 | 2000 | 3000 | Feet |
| 0 | 450 | | 900 | Meters |

Railway Station

Jarrett Park

SUNSET DR.

HOWARD COOKE HWY.

Montego River

COCONUT DR.

CALYPSO DR.

SOUTHERN CROSS BLVD.

Pies River

To Negril

If you venture nowhere else beyond the party atmosphere of Montego Bay, consider the day-long Governor's Coach tour, also known as the Catadupa Choo Choo. You ride from MoBay some 40 miles into the mountainous interior in a railroad coach that used to be the private saloon car of Jamaican governors, a calypso band and bar on board. Stops include the Appleton Rum works at Maggotty, the Ipswich Caves, and the Cockpit Country village of Catadupa, where local seamstresses will fit you for a shirt or dress, then deliver the finished product on your way back. This special excursion is run by Jamaica Tours (952–2887) and departs at 9:30 A.M. from Montego Bay railroad station Tuesday through Friday. A ticket is about $32 per person, including lunch and rum punch. Make reservations early.

Another satisfying rail trip is aboard a diesel running daily between MoBay and the capital city of Kingston. The four-and-a-half-hour trip costs only about $5 for first class (weekends only), $3 coach, one way. See a lot of interesting country in half the time (at roughly half the fare) by getting off at the town of Williamsfield; a 15-minute bus or taxi ride takes you to the town of Mandeville. If you'd rather let someone else handle the arrangements, Premier Tours (952–5919) hosts a Thursday 7 A.M. pick-up at your hotel and train ride to the Appleton Rum works, with a bus tour of Mandeville. A fare of about $45 includes breakfast, seven-course lunch at the Hotel Astra in Mandeville, rum punch, and entertainment en route.

Rather travel by water? At the Martha Brae River in Falmouth, 23 miles east of Montego Bay on Route A1, you can hire a bamboo raft for two, poled by an experienced raftsman. Start upriver at the Rafter's Village (follow the signs off the coast highway), which has a restaurant, bar, and shops. The leisurely trip toward the sea takes an hour and a half and costs about $12 per person (afterwards, you'll be driven back to your starting point). If you wish, make all the arrangements, including transportation from MoBay and back, at your hotel tour desk.

"Up, Up and Buffet" is a day tour that begins with pick-up at your hotel, a trip to a former banana plantation and breakfast, a tethered balloon ride, roast suckling pig lunch, tour of the village of Seaford Town, a German settlement, and more. The whole package costs about $48 per person ($38 without the balloon ride). Contact Hilton High (952–3343), Box 313, Montego Bay.

Would-be Indiana Joneses may wish to brave the untamed Cockpit Country. It's here that the descendants of the fierce Maroons—former slaves of the Spanish—and other "free coloureds" fought such a successful guerrilla war against the British that they won self-rule in a 1735 treaty that continues to this day. The "Land of Look Behind," where British colonials rode back-to-back on a single horse to avoid ambush, begins only some 15 miles from Montego Bay, at Maroon Town. Maroons no longer live here, but are concentrated around their capital of Accompong, further into the rugged interior. It's recommended that before venturing into this primitive enclave you contact the Jamaica Tourist Board office in MoBay for info about minibus tours and guides.

For a much more tranquil experience, head off to Lisa Salmon's bird sanctuary, the **Rocklands Feeding Station** (952–2009) in the village of Anchovy. Take Route A1 west to Route B8 south; it's about four miles in all. Miss Salmon, a painter and naturalist, settled here in the 1950s and has since offered safe haven to some 100 species, many of which alight daily to be fed from 3:30 P.M. till sundown. You are welcome to watch, quietly. Admission is $3 for adults, $1.50 for children, who must be four or older.

If you'd like a peek at the way Jamaica's rich lived two centuries ago, you need not travel far. Most famous —or infamous—of these restored mansions is **Rose Hall** (953–2323). Built around 1770 as the showplace of the Caribbean, its reputation is due in equal measure to the ghost said to haunt its elegant, antique-filled rooms. A few years back, thousands of onlookers watched as psychics tried to make contact with Annie Palmer, the second mistress of Rose Hall, who supposedly did in three husbands, as well as a plantation overseer and any number of slaves who were her lovers; she herself was murdered in her bed in 1833. (If this sounds the stuff of fiction, find a copy of Jamaican novelist Herbert deLisser's *The White Witch of Rose Hall.*)

The furnishings at Rose Hall, though many are of museum quality, are not original. And a small restaurant and bar has been added (near the torture chamber). In short, this is the most show-bizzy of the great houses in the area, but still definitely worth a look-see. It commands a ridge just beyond the Half Moon resort on Route A1, seven miles east of Montego Bay. Open every day from 9 A.M. to 6 P.M. Admission is $5 for adults, $3 for children.

If you have time, look for the side road at the edge of Rose Hall. A walled cemetery a few hundred yards down is the family plot for relatives of poet Elizabeth Barrett Browning, whose father was born at Cinnamon Hill Great House further along this road. Not open to the public, this restored mansion is owned today by country-and-western singer Johnny Cash. A bit further, ask a local "guide" to show you the waterfall used in the James Bond movie *Live and Let Die*.

Back on Route A1, about 15 miles east of MoBay, is **Greenwood** (no phone), another great house built by the Barretts, who once owned all the land from Rose Hall to Falmouth. Now owned by Bob and Ann Betton, who will share the many legends that have grown up around the property, the house has Barrett Family portraits and the family Wedgwood china, as well as a fine library with books dating from 1697 and a collection of rare music boxes and musical instruments. Greenwood is open daily from 10 A.M. to 6 P.M.; admission is about $4.

FALMOUTH

This is a picturesque sugar port of Georgian homes and broad streets. It makes for a pleasant excursion for visitors staying in either Montego Bay (23 miles east) or Ocho Rios (44 miles west), but is also a worthy island address in itself—especially for those wanting to stake out a quieter, less crowded claim on the north shore. And because of its central location, it's easy to explore the coastline in both directions.

LODGING

There's only one resort we recommend in Falmouth, but the **Trelawny Beach Hotel** (954–2450), Box 54, Falmouth, offers as much value as any on the island. Set amid pleasant gardens, this 350-room, seven-story hostelry has both private beachfront and a large pool. The lobby and other public areas are attractive and airy.

Activities abound, and most are free, including scuba (one free tank dive per day), snorkeling, Sunfish sailing, windsurfing, water-skiing, glass-bottom boat rides, tennis and tennis instruction (on four Laykold courts), reggae dance and craft classes, and live entertainment nightly. There's also a daily free shuttle service to Montego Bay, cruises on the hotel's 40-foot sailboat, and a discount on food, drink, and fishing charters at Falmouth Yacht Club.

Guests choose between two meal plans—either all meals included, or just breakfast and dinner. If this is beginning to sound like another of Jamaica's popular all-inclusive hotels, that's *almost* right. Liquor is not included in the room rate, which makes this a favorite for families. In fact, there's a daily schedule of children's activities, with specially designated hotel personnel to supervise them; baby sitters are also easily booked. In summer, children (14 years and under) stay and eat for free when accompanied by an adult. At the same time, honeymoon and wedding (the hotel arranges for a justice of the peace, marriage license, and witnesses) packages are also popular here. There is no age restriction or required minimum stay. All this adds up to what the Trelawny Beach calls the "inclusive resort for everyone."

All rooms are air-conditioned and have a private balcony or patio. Double occupancy costs $107 per person, including tax and gratuities, with two meals daily; $117 per person with three meals. Except in summer, add $20 extra per day for each child. The hotel has 40 cottage units that are especially good for families. Finaly, inquire about package deals that include airfare—these can make a stay here amazingly inexpensive.

EXPLORING

Most of Falmouth was built in the late 1700s, and its fine Georgian architecture is shown off to best advantage on Market Street, just west of Water Square at the center of town. Note especially the **Methodist Manse,** a stone-and-wood house with wrought-iron balconies built in 1799. From the square you can admire one of the best Georgian buildings in Jamaica—it's now used by the town council.

An appointment should be made to visit **Good Hope Estate** (954–3289), in the hills above town, but it's well worth it. This 18th-century sugar plantation, once home to one of the richest planters in Jamaican history, has a number of fascinating and fully restored buildings to explore, including the main house and slave prison, and wonderfully scenic gardens on 6,000 acres that can be toured on horseback (about $15 for a two-hour ride). Take the road south from Falmouth to Martha Brae, where the road forks; bear right, and when, soon, the road forks again, go left. Admission to the estate is about $5.

It's in Martha Brae—named for an Arawak Indian girl gifted, it's said, with supernatural powers—that you can hire a bamboo raft and river guide for an hour's leisurely float toward the sea.

East on Route A1, shortly before the Trelawny Beach, is a speck on the map known as Rock. There's a phosphorescent lagoon here where tiny organisms in the water glisten at night when the water is roiled; fishing charters also leave from here. Another eight miles east, at Duncans, a right onto Route B10 will take you to the **Long Pond Sugar Factory and Distillery** (954–2401), where Gold Label Rum is made; tours are available by appointment. Below Clark's Town, another right turn, at Kinloss, brings you to the outskirts of the Cockpit Country.

Back on A1, it's six more miles from Duncans to Rio Bueno (you can also reach it from Clark's Town by taking Route B11 east to B5 north), a quaint fishing village on a horseshoe-shaped harbor with a photogenic waterfront church, old stone houses, and the ruins of Fort Dundas, built in 1778. Some historians believe Christopher Columbus made his first landing on the island here in 1494.

Six miles further is Discovery Bay, so named because it has long claimed to be the site of Columbus's first landing, though the revisionist school of thought holds that he dropped anchor here on his fourth and final voyage, in 1503. In any event, Columbus Park offers an open-air museum where cannons and relics from sugar mills are on display on a limestone cliff overlooking the bay. The business of the bay these days is bauxite. Should you wish, guided tours of the **Kaiser bauxite mine and plant** (973–2221) can be arranged by appointment.

RUNAWAY BAY

With the sun-dappled sea to your left, sugar-cane fields, pasture lands, and mountain vistas to your right, the north-shore drive continues. Goats and chickens forage at the highway's edge, Jamaicans go about their everyday business, and every few miles the auto traffic slows as another town looms into view.

LODGING

About an hour's drive from the Montego Bay airport and some 27 miles past Falmouth, Runaway Bay is a cluster of several hotels. Newly rechristened the **Jack Tar Runaway Bay** (973–3404), Box 112, Runaway Bay, the former Eaton Hall Great House lends an aura of history to the all-inclusive format. It has its lovely piece of the beach, making all water sports accessible—and, like all food, drink, and just about everything else, they're included in the basic rate.

The hotel, built on the foundations of an old English fort, boasts an underground passage to the cliffs. In all, there are only 56 guest rooms; with all the extras, they rent for $260 per night for two.

Next comes the intriguing **Jamaica Jamaica** (973–2436), Box 58, Runaway Bay. As the name implies, here's the place to "do as the Jamaicans do," but on a grand scale. The music, the parties, the food—all have gone native. This, too, is an all-inclusive property and is limited to adults (over age 16). The freebies include romantic horse-and-buggy rides and a "kit and caboodle"—Jamaican-made shorts, shirt, and other gifts in a cotton duffel bag.

There's a waterfall, Jacuzzi, lap pool, and exercise room—and that's just in the lobby area, which also has a bar, shops, and more. Many of the guest rooms have been given outlandishly large bath tubs. What else is there to do? There's the beach-cum-bar, tennis, an 18-hole golf course at a nearby country club, and if that's not enough, shopping and sightseeing shuttles.

Week-long stays (minimum) are about $145 a night per person.

Now for something completely different: The **Silver Spray Club** (973–3413), Box 16, Runaway Bay, is quiet, small, and there's nary a planned activity in sight. What else does it offer? The beach. A nice pool. Good food. A loyal clientele. The 19 cottage-like rooms on the beach go for about $65 a night.

EXPLORING

The most famous sightseeing stop hereabouts is **Runaway Caves** (follow the signs west of the bay), where fleeing slaves once hid and where today guides escort visitors through strangely beautiful limestone caverns and across eerie Green Grotto Lake, 120 feet below ground. Open 9 A.M. to 5 P.M. daily, except Sunday; admission is $3 for adults, $1.50 for children.

Some 10 miles east (look for signs near the intersections of Routes A1 and A3) is the little town of St. Ann's Bay. Black nationalist hero Marcus Garvey was born here in 1887, and his monument presides in front of the town library. Just east of town is **Drax Hall,** where England's Prince Charles has played polo and Jamaicans do likewise.

OCHO RIOS

Ocho Rios is an overgrown, fun-loving village fringed by a ribbon of white sand. It is both a great place to stay and a great place to stop—it is also the island's foremost cruise-ship destination.

LODGING

A particularly special place, in the hills above St. Ann's Bay, seven miles west of Ocho Rios, is the 51-acre **High Hope Estate** (972–2277; reservations 818–706–1897) which, with its black wrought iron on white walls, graceful arches, and finely maintained grounds, resembles a 15th-century Venetian villa. The beach is a short drive away, but there's a pool on the premises—as well as an accommodating staff that will prepare your meals (plus a daily tea) and tend to other needs. Ten people can share the place for $4,900 a week; it will accommodate as many as 14 people at $5,500 a week. A package rate of $950 a week per person includes airport transfers, a van to drive, all food and drinks, plus tips for the staff.

About a five-minute drive west of Ocho Rios is another of the island's converts to the couples-only, all-inclusive plan. **Eden II** (972–2300), Mammee Bay, Box 51, Ocho Rios, was a member of the Hilton family for most of its life, but now has been renovated and reincarnated as an Americana Hotels property. From the rush of the waterfall in the plant-bedecked lobby to the daily theme parties (Caribbean Carnival Night, Reggae Beach Party, et al.), this is an action address. It boasts a lovely beach and complimentary water sports (including scuba) to match, a pool, five tennis courts, fitness center, horseback riding, golf (prepaid at a nearby course)—plus the usual surfeit of food, drinks, and tobacco products. With one of its 265 rooms, each with private balcony, all this goes for about $1,150 per person for four days, three nights; $2,100 for seven days, six nights.

If it's the big, boisterous, and no-surprises atmosphere of a mass-market hotel you seek, the **Ocho Rios Sheraton** (974–2201; toll-free 800–325–3535), Box 245, Ocho Rios, is your kind of place. Especially, we'd add, if there's an attractive package deal available. Largest resort in town, it has everything you'd expect: beach, pool, tennis courts, volleyball, Ping-Pong, health club, shops, disco, two restaurants, bar, and coffee shop. It's also within walking distance of the Ocean Village Shopping Centre and neighboring beachfront hostelries.

The Sheraton's 394 rooms start at $130 double; one-bedroom suites go for about $250 a night.

Talk about good neighbors: Just up the beach, the **Americana Ocho Rios** (974–2151), Box 100, Ocho Rios, is the Sheraton's virtual twin in terms of style, approach, and amenities. Here, again, look for the right package deal, then enjoy this 11-story tower's five restaurants (the Victoria is fanciest), two swimming pools, tennis courts, and primo location. Its 325 air-conditioned rooms start at around $110 for a double and top out at $125.

A world apart but actually just beyond Mallards Bay is the homey **Hibiscus Lodge** (974–2676), Main Street, Box 52, Ocho Rios. You're still within a short stroll of the center of town, restaurants, and shopping, but the mood is far removed from the big-name hotels and steamy couples resorts. This is a destination favored by savvy Europeans, and it's easy to see why. Golfers have entrée to Upton Country Club south of town. And even though the lodge itself is on the captivatingly blue water, it is more reminiscent of Capri than the Caribbean. A stone staircase leads down a 30-foot cliff to a spit of sand that is protected by a reef ideal for snorkeling; the kitchen of the lodge's extremely popular, open-air Almond Tree restaurant is presided over by a Swiss-born chef.

Here is the place to hide or seek, at your pleasure. The inn's 21 rooms are modern and comfortable, have private baths, and all overlook the sea. Best of all, they rent in the $80-per-night range.

About two miles east of the center of town, on the coastal Route A3, the **Plantation Inn** (974–2501), Box 2, Ocho Rios, sits on 10 splendid acres of tropical hillside and white-sand beach. Without question among the finest resorts in the Caribbean, this elegant retreat has been satisfying visitors with discriminating taste for more than three decades by providing uncommonly high standards of service and comfort. Breakfast is served in the privacy of your room balcony. Mid-afternoon tea is a daily ritual. And dinner is a gourmet affair followed by dancing on the starlit veranda.

The beach—actually twin crescents of sand—is a climb down flower-edged steps. Water sports are superb. For diving, there's a spectacular technicolor reef 100 yards offshore. There are also two tennis courts, a pool, and shops (and a shopping center just beyond the front gates).

Impeccably furnished, the 65 guest rooms range from about $270 to $310 a night, while suites go for $325. Breakfasts and dinners are included.

Another grand old seat of hospitality shares Sandy Beach Bay. Just a short distance further along the coast route is the polished brass plaque on a stone pillar announcing the entrance to the small, classic **Jamaica Inn** (974–2514; toll-free 800–243–9420), Box 1, Ocho Rios. Service and surroundings have built up a loyal clientele since the inn opened in 1951, and often it's difficult for a newcomer to find a vacancy although it's worth a try.

The inn is perched on a cliff above a private paradise of beach, where Sunfish and snorkel gear are available for rentals. A rum punch from a white-jacketed waiter is yours for the asking—compliments of the house—while you sun. Tennis on the premises; riding and golf (at Upton Country Club) are quickly arranged. The Continental and local cuisine in the dining room is excellent.

Each of the 50 lovely rooms has a private veranda suitable either for splendid isolation or entertaining friends. The stay is worth it, even at from $250 to $300 a night, including breakfast and dinner.

The **Shaw Park Beach** (974–2552), Box 17, Ocho Rios, about two-and-a-half miles east of town, is a popular hotel among Europeans and small tour groups. The Silks disco here is a local hangout. There's the usual complement of activities—water sports off a restful beach, tennis, pool, and the like. The 118 air-conditioned rooms are strung out in two-story units and start at around $150 a night double.

Pastel-pink and white buildings terrace down a lush hillside to private Little Bay at the **Sans Souci Hotel and Club** (974–2353), Box 103, Ocho Rios. About four miles east of the town center on Route A3, the Sans Souci is nothing short of a tropical oasis.

Day begins with breakfast served on your private balcony, which is angled for a stunning sea view. Then perhaps it's off to the beachfront water sports center for sailing, snorkeling, water-skiing, diving, or a fishing trip; or to the tennis club for one of the two Laykold courts. How about a round of golf at nearby Upton Country Club instead? Horseback riding? Polo? If you'd rather relax at poolside, take your pick. In addition to its fresh-water pool, there's also a natural, spring-fed pool whose waters have a mineral content comparable to that at spas of Europe.

For dining in style, the award-winning Casanova restaurant is arguably the best in Ocho Rios. For those who are do-it-yourselfers, the suites come with kitchenettes. All 80 stylish units are air-conditioned and also have ceiling fans. Rates start at $200 a night; a one-bedroom suite is about $250. For an additional $45 a person, breakfast, dinner, and most drinks are included.

Couples (974–4271), Tower Isle, St. Mary, is some 20 minutes' drive east along the north shore past Ocho Rios. This is the place that began the Club Med-like, adults-only, all-inclusive craze on the island in 1978. And its popularity is attested to by the highest occupancy rate of any resort in Jamaica. Little wonder. It seems the management has thought of everything—and *everything* is included in the weekly rate.

The list is long: all meals, including liquor and midnight snacks, cigarettes, talent shows, disco and reggae dancing, all manner of water sports (including deep-sea fishing and scuba), Nautilus gym, tennis, pool, nude and non-nude beaches, volleyball, Ping-Pong, yoga, bicycling . . . there's more, but you get the idea.

All 152 cheerful rooms have private bath, air-conditioning, a private balcony or patio. Figure on about $2,100 per couple for seven days, six nights in peak season. Remember, no children or solitary travelers are allowed.

EXPLORING

Dunn's River Falls (974–2857) and beach, a few miles west of Ocho Rios, is *the* must-see along this stretch of the north shore. And it is indeed one of Jamaica's chief natural wonders—a clear mountain stream that cascades in tiers for 600 feet to a pristine beach and the sea. The thing is to climb . . . splash . . . to the top, an arduous but exhilarating experience. You can do it on your own, joining in the human daisy chain that gingerly works its way up; or you can hire a guide who knows the slippery spots and will safeguard your camera and snap your photo as you climb.

A bathing suit is the proper uniform for this mini-adventure. There are changing facilities here, as well as snack bars and souvenir sellers. Stairs lead down a tunnel under Route A1 to the beach, where you can rent a locker for your valuables. Then you must buy a ticket—for about 50 cents, available daily during daylight hours—to make the climb.

A three-mile stretch of Route A3 south of town is known as Fern Gully, in which the road snakes down an old riverbed that is shaded by the lush, cool green of giant ferns. Watch for **Shaw Park Gardens** on a hilltop west of the roadway (the Ruins restaurant is just below); there are 34 acres with gorgeous views of Ocho Rios below, pretty ponds and meandering streams, as well as many tagged varieties of trees and flowers. Perfect for a quiet stroll or picnic.

Should you be in the mood for a longer excursion, the southern route (Route A3 to A1) through the interior—over Mount Diablo and through the awesome gorge of Bog Walk—leads to Spanish Town and the capital city of Kingston. The total distance is 58 miles, but figure driving time of one-and-a-half to two hours.

East of the center of Ocho Rios, near the White River, is a sign pointing to the route inland to **Prospect Estate** (974–2058), a working banana and cassava plantation that offers guided tours. Open daily, except Sunday, from 9 A.M. to 5 P.M.; admission is about $6 for adults, $3 for children.

A short way further along the coast highway (Route A3) is **Harmony Hall** (974–4222), a restored 19th-century great house that houses a gallery displaying Jamaican arts and crafts, as well as a bar and restaurant. It's open every day from 10 A.M. to 6 P.M.

Thirteen miles east of Ocho Rios is the village of Oracabessa. Watch for the Esso station. Take the narrow lane nearby leading toward the sea; you'll come upon a beach lined with old-style dugout canoes and gateposts topped by carved wooden pineapples. This is **Golden Eye**, the villa owned for nearly two decades by Ian Fleming, author of the James Bond novels, and later by reggae legend Bob Marley. Other literary lights, including Truman Capote and Graham Greene, have escaped winter here. It's not open to public view, alas.

While we're of a literary bent, let's proceed still further eastward on the main coast road. Before reaching Port Maria, on your right, a sign directs you up a dirt road to the hilltop aerie of the late, great master of drawing-room wit—British playwright, author, and composer Noel Coward. Sir Noel's books, records, manuscripts, even his clothes closets are as he left them when he died in this simple house in 1973. Known as **Firefly** (no phone), it now belongs to the National Trust of Jamaica and is maintained as a museum and memorial. Coward's grave is behind his home, which is open daily, except Sunday, from 10 A.M. to 5 P.M.; admission is $1.

Route B13 from Port Maria soon leads to **Brimmer Hall** (no phone), where you ride an open-air jitney through pimento (allspice), banana, and coconut groves. This working plantation has a great house for inspection, where a tasty lunch can also be had. It's open Monday through Saturday from 9 A.M. to 5 P.M.; admission is about $6 for adults, $3 for children.

PORT ANTONIO

Beautiful and unspoiled, Port Antonio is still nearly the secret hideaway it once was for film stars Clara Bow, Bette Davis, Erroll Flynn, and Ginger Rogers—not to mention J.P. Morgan, when he was the richest man in the world. Celebrities and an in-the-know elite continue to seek it out, but you don't have to be famous to share the wealth.

Getting here takes a bit of doing—it's almost a four-hour drive from either Kingston or Montego Bay. (You can, however, take an inter-island flight from either city's airport to Ken Jones Airfield west of town.) But the effort is rewarded with a demure fishing village huddled around twin harbors, surrounded by Jamaica's lushest and most romantic countryside—and the chance to revel in what has been aptly described as "the most exquisite port on earth."

LODGING

Pleasant accommodations for the budget-minded are scarce in Port Antonio, but best of the lot is the **Bonnie View** (993–2752), Box 82, Port Antonio. On a street of the same name that begins in the center of town, this hilltop hotel offers spectacular views, an impressive pool and sundeck, and a restaurant that serves tasty, homestyle island fare. Some of the 30 rooms have private balconies with a sensational view; all are adequate and rent at about $65 double.

Some three miles east of the village, on the coast road (Route A4), is the superb **Trident Villas and Hotel** (993–2602; toll-free 800–235–3505; in New York 212–689–3048), Box 119, Port Antonio. Rebuilt after Hurricane Allen leveled the place a few years back, it is, if anything, better than ever—and still a favorite hideaway for European and Hollywood royalty alike. But anyone can enjoy Trident's elegant charms. It's set on 17 acres of dramatic, palm-fringed coastline, with peacocks strutting the lawns, and regal service—white-gloved and deferential. There is a lovely swimming pool that overlooks the sea, as well as a small private beach for water sports; a pair of tennis courts, too. Mrs. Errol Flynn has a small boutique here.

The main attractions at the Trident, though, are its dining room and the accommodations themselves. The former, with cut crystal, shining silver, and dress code (jacket and tie at dinner during the winter season, jacket only at other times), may be the best on the island, if not the entire Caribbean. Off the candlelit dining room is a cozy bar and intimate sitting room—the feel overall of a very special, private European villa.

Breakfast can be taken (one course at a time) on your private balcony or veranda that faces the sea. Each of the 28 antique-furnished suites is distinctive and unique, with Jamaican-made replicas of antiques, ceiling fans to circulate sea breezes, a sitting room, and pantry. Count on serenity—no TV or radio. These beauties range from $295 to $480 a night, double, including breakfast and dinner.

Further east of town, **Frenchman's Cove** (993–3224), Box 101, Port Antonio, earned its reputation more than two decades ago as a pricey paradise ("two people spent $2,000 for two weeks!" the hotel boasted) to the stars. Today, the celebs seek out new venues, and the prices aren't so steep anymore, yet these classic resort houses made of stone and set on 44 lush and tropical acres are still favored by vacationing islanders and others who seek a private, pristine escape from it all. The sandy beach at the cove is particularly scenic, and if you prefer splashing in fresh water, river swimming is right there, too.

Each of the houses comes with a housekeeper who cooks and does laundry. Your link to the main hotel, its dining room, and the beach beyond is your own golf cart. The all-inclusive rate in a villa suite (a rental car with a seven-day stay) is about $160 per person; with room and breakfast only, about $100. In one of the hotel rooms, it's $85 a night, all-inclusive; or about $45 with just bed and breakfast.

On a hill overlooking San San Bay about six miles east of Port Antonio, the villas at **Goblin Hill** (993– 3286), San San, Port Antonio, are ideal for families or others wanting hotel amenities with a private-home atmosphere. White stucco buildings sit on sprawling, verdant grounds with glorious views of the bay. The beach is down the hill, and so it's a short drive to snorkeling and sand, but a pool is close at hand, as well as two night-lighted tennis courts. Other activities—water-skiing, scuba, horseback riding, and more—can be arranged.

Each townhouse-like villa comes equipped with a maid to handle the cooking and housekeeping. A liquor store and commissary are also on the grounds. The dozen one-bedroom units go for $1,080 per week; the 16 two-bedrooms are $1,680. All include airport transfers and a car.

EXPLORING

What's to see and do in Port Antonio? Well, you can poke around the gingerbready village, enjoy the lush tropical green that all but envelopes you, or the beaches, or the sea—deep-sea fishing is excellent here—or . . . . One of the area's charms, to many, is that it is pretty much unspoiled and undeveloped, from a tourist's standpoint. So relax and enjoy.

Not that there aren't local sights worth finding. It's here, for example, that you can enjoy the best, and original, raft trip in Jamaica. Local lore has it that film star Errol Flynn started it all when he noticed the long, thin bamboo rafts being used to transport bananas down the Rio Grande River for shipping. Today, embarking from Berrydale, southwest of Port Antonio, a skilled raftman (and often a skilled storyteller) will guide you on an idyllic three-hour voyage to the sea; along the way, your two-passenger conveyance may pause to allow you to splash in a quiet pool, or you can dangle a fishing line, or enjoy the picnic lunch you packed. Vendors sell Red Stripe beer and Cokes along the way—or you can hold out till you reach Rafters Rest, on St. Margaret's Bay at journey's end, where a bar, restaurant, and souvenir shopping await. The leisurely excursion costs about $45 per raft. For information, contact Rio Rafting (993–2626), 7 Harbour Street, Port Antonio.

East of Port Antonio's east harbor, on a headland, sits the remains of a vast classical structure known hereabouts as **Folly,** built in 1905 by a Connecticut jeweler named Alfred Mitchell. His wife was a Tiffany, and they lived here until Mitchell's death in 1912. Just east of the Trident Hotel, architect Earl Levy (who owns the Trident) has been working several years to complete a fantasy castle that looks straight out of a child's storybook; ask at the hotel if it's open for viewing.

Just east of San San Bay, follow the signs to the **Blue Hole**—the Blue Lagoon, to those who saw the movie of the same name that was partially filmed here. More recently, this was the setting for another Hollywood tale, *Club Paradise.* Its intensely blue waters are estimated to reach down some 180 feet.

On a road that arcs south from Port Antonio and back to the coast at Fairy Hill are the caves of **Nonsuch,** popular with both serious spelunkers and the just plain adventuresome for their fossilized sea life, coral, and remnants of an early Arawak Indian community. Local guides are eager to help, for a small, negotiable fee.

Near Priestman's River, a few miles east of Boston Bay—*the* place to sample jerk pork or chicken, an aromatic barbecue invented centuries ago by the freed slaves known as Maroons—lies the 2,000-acre ranch owned by Patrice Wymore Flynn, Errol's widow. Horseback riding is special here, and tours are offered at times, especially when cruise ships are in port. Make arrangements through your hotel, or leave word for Mrs. Flynn at her boutique at the Trident Hotel (993–3294).

The drive from Priestman's River along the coast (Route A4) to the town of Manchioneal is splendid—as scenic, many say, as the famed Hana Highway on the Hawaiian island of Maui. Just past Manchioneal, take the turnoff before the Driver's River bridge and detour inland for a mile or until the bumpy road forks. A crude sign will direct you to **Reach Falls**, one of the most spectacular waterfalls in all Jamaica—and one of the least visited. Stone stairs—watch your step!—lead to the bottom of the falls; then, if you wish, take a peak at the caves under the falls.

Kingston

Strange to say, but this bustling metropolitan area of 700,000, most populous by far on the island and largest English-speaking city south of Miami, is often overlooked by other than business travelers. The capital of Jamaica since 1872, it is also the seat of island commerce and culture. The old pirate enclave of Port Royal is just across the harbor, and the beauty and serenity of the 7,000-foot Blue Mountains are but a breathtaking drive away. By auto, Kingston is about four hours from Montego Bay, under three hours from Port Antonio, and under two from Ocho Rios. For a break from basking on a beach—and especially if you want to look into the heart of this fascinating Caribbean nation—do sample Kingston.

The centerpiece of the capital these days is the area known as New Kingston, once a race track, and now a gleaming mix of hotels, restaurants, theaters, boutiques, as well as office towers and apartments. It is here that you will find the attractive Tourism Centre Building, at 21 Dominica Drive, home of the Jamaica Tourist Board; it's your one-stop headquarters for answers or assistance regarding any locale or activity on the island.

LODGING

The city boasts several of the island's finest hotels. Remember that room rates listed here are in U.S. currency before tax and service charge (subject to fluctuations in the exchange rate, of course), and that from mid-April to mid-December, these drop as much as half.

Near the Tourism Centre Building is the **Wyndham New Kingston** (926–5430; toll-free 800–822–4200), 85 Knutsford Boulevard. After a dazzling refurbishment by the Dallas-based Wyndham hotel group, it's become a solid hit with business and pleasure travelers alike. The first impression is tropical and expansive, with a lobby that is airy and accented with wicker and greenery. A 17-story tower and seven cabana buildings curl around the Olympic-sized pool and landscaped grounds, where macaws screech and the hubbub of the city is lost.

There's plenty to do here. Besides the pool, there's a health club, library, and tennis privileges at the night-lit Liguanea Club across the street. The hotel's Ristorante D'Amore sounds romantic and Italian, and it is both— with spectacular roof-top views of the city, the bay, and the mountains beyond. The breezy, open-air Cafe Macaw is perfect for a leisurely breakfast or lunch. In a party mood? Then head for the Jonkanoo Lounge.

The Wyndham has a total of 400 spacious rooms, all air-conditioned, though those in the tower are newer and afford the better views. Doubles range from $95 to $105, while those wanting the "ultraservice" of the "presidential" floors (14 through 16)—a private lounge and other extras—pay $120 a night.

Practically next door is another splendidly renovated hostelry, the **Jamaica Pegasus** (926–3691; toll-free from the U.S. 800–223–5672), 81 Knutsford Boulevard. Here, the mood is elegant and upscale, with marble floors and pastel hues in the lobby, where you can find some of the best duty-free shopping on the island. Just off the lobby is the graceful Le Pavillion, noted for its high teas, as well as elegant dining; and the Surrey Tavern, which serves up pub grub and, frequently, first-rate jazz, making it a popular Kingston nightspot.

Going up? The Talk of the Town, which sits atop the hotel on the 17th floor, has both city views and one of the most ambitious kitchens in town.

Going down? One level below the lobby is the pool bar and a dependable coffee shop, overlooking a sizeable kidney-shaped pool with a three-tiered fountain gurgling at one end. This is the setting for the weekly manager's cocktail party, replete with tasty island snacks, a bartender with a generous nature, and a lively calypso band. The pool and gardens are ringed by a jogger's track, and there is a health club, two new floodlit all-weather tennis courts, and a shallow children's pool.

Each of the 350 attractively appointed rooms is air-conditioned, has satellite TV and a private balcony with a mountain or sea view. From the front desk attendant to the maid, the mood is helpful and efficient, and the 24-hour room service is fast and surprisingly reasonable (how about a pizza for about $3, or a steaming bowl of spicy Jamaican pepperpot soup for less than $1?).

Rates are about $130 for a double. The Pegasus is also a favored business address, and so its Knutsford Club floors (14 through 16) feature extras such as check-in facilities directly on the floor, private lounges, complimentary cocktail hours, and business services. Doubles here go for about $145.

At harborside, hard by the convention center, National Gallery, and government offices is another modern high-rise, the **Hotel Oceana Kingston** (922–0920; toll-free 800–221–4588), 2 King Street. Built as a member of the Inter-Continental hotel chain, this is a business and convention destination primarily, though its splendid waterfront vista, pool, beauty salon, shopping arcade, and cocktail lounge with live entertainment make it a pleasurable stopover for anyone visiting the capital. The ferry to Port Royal across the bay is nearby, and the eager-to-please hotel staff can also arrange for fishing, boating, or golf outings.

The 152 air-conditioned rooms all have TVs, are pleasantly appointed and modern. Ask for a harbor view.

Double or single, they are about $90 in high season; suites range from $100 to $500 per night.

The Courtleigh (926–8174), 31 Trafalgar Road, is a mid-sized hostelry with the feel of a fine country club. Impeccable white buildings with well-tended greenery is the look without; white with accents of color predominates within. The pool area, with its umbrella-shaded tables and shingle-roofed bar, is especially restful. You'll likely meet visiting Britons relaxing here, sipping at their gin and tonics and discoursing on cricket-league standings. The open-air Plantation Terrace hosts a civilized lunch, while a bar called Mingles is a favored evening destination. The Courtleigh's nicely appointed rooms start at around $65, with a three-bedroom suite costing $145.

Two erstwhile private residences offer a more homey stay. The **Mayfair** (926–1610), 4 West Kings House Close, is set on a lovely cul-de-sac near historic Devon House. The impressive main guest house has a pool and patio for use by all—as well as for locally renowned Wednesday and Saturday buffets—while the surrounding homes have been converted into rooms for hire.

This is a particular favorite of visitors from Britain and Europe, though hostess Sybil Hughes goes the extra mile to help all her guests enjoy both her hotel and the island. Expect to pay $40 to $50 double occupancy; all guest rooms are air-conditioned and have private bath. You'll need to depend on taxis or a car to explore the city from here.

The main part of the **Terra Nova Hotel** (926–9334), 17 Waterloo Road, had its origins as a balustraded private home set amid manicured gardens. There's a seldom-busy pool and a restaurant popular among the Jamaican business, government, and capital-society sets; after dark, its nightclub is a favorite spot among Kingstonian professionals.

The 30 rooms are all air-conditioned and the rate, single or double, is about $70 per night. Since this hotel is also in a residential neighborhood, you'll need transportation to get around.

How about a few days or more of splendid isolation?

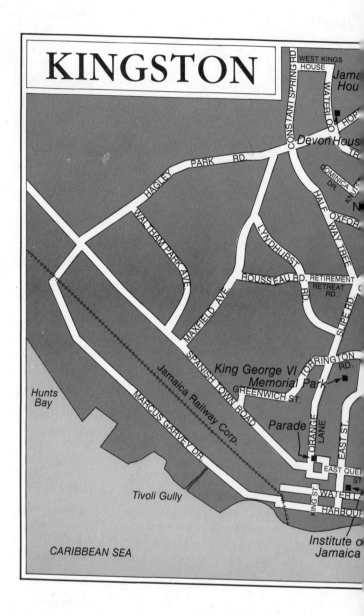

KINGSTON

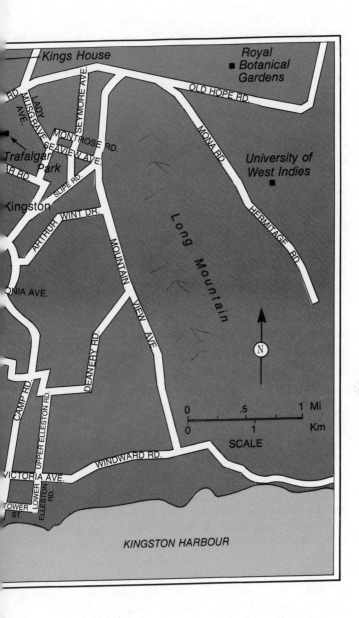

Kings House

Royal Botanical Gardens

OLD HOPE RD.

RD.
LADY MUSGRAVE AVE.
SEYMORE AVE.
MONTROSE RD.
SEAVIEW AVE.

MONA RD.

University of West Indies

Trafalgar Park

8H RD.

Kingston

SLIPE RD.

ARTHUR WINT DR.

HERMITAGE RD.

Long Mountain

ONIA AVE.

MOUNTAIN VIEW AVE.

DEANERY RD.

N

CAMP RD.

UPPER ELLESTON RD.

0   .5   1 Mi
0   1   Km
SCALE

WINDWARD RD.

VICTORIA AVE.

LOWER ELLESTON RD.

TOWER ST.

KINGSTON HARBOUR

High above the city in the scenic Blue Mountains sits **Pine Grove Chalets** (922–8705); mailing address, 29 Olivier Place, Kingston. This is coffee-growing country, and this small lodge-like establishment—owned since the late 1970s by one of Jamaica's most prominent lawyers—is in the midst of a coffee plantation; it's refreshingly cool and lush up here, and the vistas are spectacular. In short, this is close to heaven for both lovers of solitude and lovers seeking solitude; many who stay here hike or climb the surrounding mountains.

The down-home staff will prepare three delicious meals a day upon request—and the fare in the simple but attractive dining room or patio terrace, where the view is top-of-the-world, is both tasty and inexpensive. The 17 no-frills guest rooms all have refrigerators and cooking facilities, and televisions are available at extra charge; no phones in the rooms. They range from studios at about $30 a night to a one-bedroom cottage for only $35; extra beds are $2 apiece.

One proviso: The 45-minute drive up from Kingston is not for the timid, what with many mountain switchbacks and rutted roadbed. The hotel will pick you up at the airport, if you make the arrangements in advance.

Finally, if even in a city as vibrant as Kingston you can't bear the thought of Jamaica without a beach, here's your solution: **Morgan's Harbour** (924–8464) on Main Road in Port Royal. The skyline of Kingston lies directly across the harbor, and is accessible in minutes by ferry. Norman Manley Airport is a short drive away; historic Port Royal, the ruined pirate enclave, is but a short hike. And the hotel itself is a port of call. Yachts bob in their berths just yards from the hotel's cafe and breeze-refreshed seaside bar—the hotel complex encompasses a yacht marina and beach club. Nearby is a cozy beach for sunning and salt-water swimming, but there's a harborside pool as well. Water-skiing, scuba, and deep-sea fishing are easily arranged. The atmosphere here is yacht-club casual, a pleasurable contrast to the more formal capital.

The rooms are in two-story wings. Smallish but clean, they are all air-conditioned and go for about $80 to $90 a night, depending on the view.

EXPLORING

Kingston is chaotic and civilized. Kingston is exuberant and discreet. Kingston is tawdry and magnificent. Kingston is past and present. Above all, Kingston is the living heart of Jamaica—and no one who wishes to understand this fascinating people and place can overlook it.

The stunning contrasts of Jamaican culture can be seen in a few hour's tour along Hope Road just north of New Kingston. Start at **Devon House** (929–6602), at the intersection of Hope and Waterloo roads. This mansion —or great house, as these preserved architectural treasures are known on the island—dates to 1881; it was built by island craftsmen for George Stiebel, one of the first black millionaires of the West Indies, who furnished it elegantly with the best Caribbean-made pieces of his day. Both the historic house and its contents were restored to their original splendor for a visit by Queen Elizabeth II in 1983, and Devon House is today one of the country's best glimpses into a remarkable past. Open Monday through Saturday from 10 A.M. to 5:30 P.M.; admission is $1.

A visit to Devon House isn't complete, however, without a stop out back, where the low buildings that form an enclosed courtyard formerly served as stables and a carriage house. Now they shelter the island's best collection of Jamaican crafts and gifts as a series of shops operated by Things Jamaican Ltd. There's also a tempting bakery and an ice-cream stand (a scoop of guava or soursop, anyone?).

Sit on benches under the protective shade of a massive mahogany and admire the courtyard's profusion of tropical flora. Or better yet, step up onto the checkerboard-tiled back porch of the great house itself, settle into a wicker chair at one of the tables of **The Coffee Terrace**, and treat yourself to a cool drink, a snack, or a full lunch or dinner.

A short distance east on Hope Road is a large park. Here, the modern **Jamaica House** was built in the 1960s as the residence of the prime minister, but today serves as the national leader's executive offices. (He lives close by on Montrose Road off Lady Musgrave Road, in a plantation house built in 1694 known as Vale Royal that has a rooftop lookout tower.) Near the center of the park is **Kings House,** official residence of the governor-general, the British crown's representative on the island. Visitors may stroll the 200 acres of tranquil parkland, but neither house is open for touring.

Just beyond the park and its official majesty, at 56 Hope Road, is a startling sight. A walled 19th-century mansion over which an Ethiopian flag flies; through the ornate iron gate is clearly visible a massive figure in dreadlocks, a guitar slung across his chest. Welcome to the **Bob Marley Museum** (927–7103), a tribute to the reggae legend.

It was here that Marley lived with his wife and five children, and where he recorded at a studio called Tuff Gong International. Today it continues to house the still-thriving Marley music empire, plus the most comprehensive collection of Marley memorabilia anywhere, documenting the musician's life from his ghetto childhood to worldwide acclaim to early death. The museum is open from 9:30 A.M. to 5 P.M. Monday, Tuesday, Thursday, and Friday; 12:30 to 5 P.M. Wednesday; and from 12:30 to 6 P.M. Saturday. It closes for lunch hour at 1:30 P.M. Admission is about $1.50 for adults, 50 cents for children.

Back on Hope Road (which becomes Old Hope Road), the next stop is **Hope Botanical Gardens,** 200 acres laid out in the 1880s on land once belonging to Major Richard Hope, who arrived with the British in 1655. Since a visit by Queen Elizabeth II in 1953, these broad lawns and lovely ornamental gardens have been known officially as the Royal Botanical Gardens, though few Kingstonians call them that. Guides are on hand to give tours, but most of the tropical flora is labeled. The Orchid House is special. Children, especially, will like the small zoo and Coconut Park, a modest funland. Open daily; free to all.

Another refuge from the hurly-burly of the city is the "You-wee" campus—the **University of the West Indies** —which extends both north and south of Old Hope Road past the botanical gardens. Its chapel, near the main entrance, is the biggest draw for visitors. "Edward Morant Gale: 1799" is inscribed at the top of the stone pediment below the roofline. Gale ran a sugar plantation in Trelawny, and this sturdy stone structure was his curing house; it was reassembled here, stone by stone. Much of the campus, in fact, sits on the site of the Mona and Papine sugarworks. Ruins of the aqueduct and sugar factory are scattered throughout the grounds.

Now head downtown, toward the waterfront. (A good route: Retracing your path, about a mile past the botanical gardens is the intersection of Hope and Old Hope roads; take a left onto Old Hope; as you near downtown, this becomes Slipe Road.) At Torrington Road, a left will bring you quickly to **National Heroes Park,** formerly a race track and now nearly 75 acres of gardens, playing fields, and memorials to Jamaican heroes.

At the corner of Orange Street (the continuation of Slipe) and Ocean Boulevard, in the Roy West Building on the waterfront, is the new home of the **National Gallery of Jamaica** (922–8540). Opened here in 1984, the gallery houses a collection spanning the island's history from colonial times onward, but is particularly impressive in the works of Jamaicans since the 1920s. Several sculptures are on exhibit by Edna Manley, the talented wife of the nation's second prime minister. Also noteworthy are the sculpture (in the indigenous hardwood, lignum vitae) and painting of Mallica Reynolds, who called himself Kapo. Open Monday through Saturday, 9:30 A.M. to 5 P.M.

A short jaunt westward is the recently refurbished **Jamaica Crafts Market** (922–3015), 52 Port Royal Street, the island's largest bazaar for handmade straw, wood, and embroidered goods—and a sightseeing stop in its own right. Many of these items are available nowhere else, so a look-see is worthwhile even if you don't realize you *need* that handsome dried calabash. Not much negotiating over price goes on here, except on more

pricey items, but as you run a gauntlet of sidewalk higglers outside, play your best version of *Let's Make a Deal.*
Open Monday through Friday from 8 A.M. to 5 P.M.; till
6 P.M. on Saturday.

The **Institute of Jamaica** (922–0620), 12 East
Street, was founded in the 1870s "for the encourage-
ment of literature, science, and art" and at this location
houses the world's largest collection of West Indian reference material in the National Library of Jamaica, as
well as a museum and herbarium in its Natural History
Division. The library, indispensable for West Indian
scholars, also contains intriguing oddities like the Shark
Papers, damning evidence tossed overboard by a guilty
sea captain and recovered years after in the belly of a
shark. The natural-history collection includes everything
from Arawak Indian carvings to living specimens of island plantlife. Open from 9:30 A.M. to 5 P.M., Monday
through Saturday.

Across from the city, at the tip of the 17-mile-long
spit of land that encloses Kingston harbor, sleeps what
was once called the wickedest city in the world. In the late
17th century, **Port Royal,** home to pirate Henry Morgan
and his Brethren of the Coast, was awash in booty robbed
from Spanish galleons on the high seas. This was a party
town—with 40 taverns to serve the lusty buccaneers and
their innumerable ladies.

In 1692 a ruinous earthquake and tidal wave ended
the party for good. But the port did not die. In the next
century this was headquarters in the West Indies for the
British Royal Navy. It was during this period that a 20-
year-old officer named Horatio Nelson, who would
become a great admiral, was in charge of the 104 guns
of Fort Charles, oldest structure in Port Royal. These
days it is a quiet fishing village with haunting echoes of
its notorious past.

The old Naval Hospital at the fort is now the **Port
Royal Archaeological and Historical Museum,** displaying centuries-old relics recovered by scuba expeditions
from the submerged area of the pirate city just offshore.
A small Maritime Museum is nearby, as is an old artillery
store known as Giddy House, at a tipsy angle thanks to
a subsequent quake in 1907. St. Peter's Church, dating

to 1754, boasts in its collection of silver platters a communion plate said to have been a gift from Morgan.

In a graveyard at the church entrance, one tombstone epitaph tells the strange-but-true tale of Lewis Galdy, "the man who died twice." The earth opened to swallow him in 1692, but another tremor spewed him into the sea, where he was rescued. "He lived many years after in Great Reputation," reads the stone; he died in 1739, at the age of 88.

All Port Royal attractions are open from 9 A.M. to 5 P.M. daily.

The Inland Island

This is the Jamaica few but Jamaicans know, the island without a beach (though nowhere are the sea and sand very far away) but with a host of intriguing byways and all-but-undiscovered charms. If you want to know the "real" Jamaica, away from the cruise-ship ports and limbo contests, discover the Inland Island.

SPANISH TOWN

Although only a half-hour drive west from Kingston, the Inland Island starts here. Although there are no hotels we'd recommend, Spanish Town makes a worthwhile stopover as you enter the Jamaican interior (or, driving down from Ocho Rios, as you approach Kingston). The city was originally laid out by a son of Christopher Columbus in the early 1500s; called Villa de la Vega, it served as the colonial capital for more than three centuries, until 1872.

First, a bit of forewarning: Spanish Town is neither

organized nor sanitized for the benefit of visitors. Streets are narrow, usually crowded with traffic and pedestrians, and confusing. And despite its rich history, most of its residents are poor. If you lack a spirit of adventure, perhaps it would be wise to stick to a guided tour (available from Kingston or Ocho Rios) or skip this stop.

EXPLORING

At the center of everything is the Plaza Mayor, the town square conceived by the Spanish, but bordered by architecture dating to British rule of the island. There's the old British House of Assembly (1762), with its long, shady colonnade, now used for local government offices; the grand portico and facade of King's House, once the governor's residence but gutted by fire in 1925; the 1819 courthouse; a cupolaed monument housing a marble statue of Admiral Rodney, the British naval commander who kept the French from seizing the island in 1782; as well as several historic Georgian houses.

On the site of King's House is a small **archaeological museum** (no phone) that displays artifacts found here. In the adjacent former stables the **Jamaica Peoples Museum of Craft and Technology** (no phone) harbors a fascinating and wide-ranging collection of relics. Both are open from 9 A.M. to 5 P.M. weekdays.

A short, five-block walk back in the direction of Kingston brings you to the site of the oldest cathedral in the Western Hemisphere. The **Cathedral Church of St. James,** on Barrett Street, was originally constructed in 1523; the brick structure with wooden steeple that stands here now dates to 1714. Don't miss the tombs and memorials, some from the 17th century.

Three miles east of town, on Route A1 to Kingston, is the **White Marl Arawak Museum** (no phone), a reconstruction of an Arawak Indian hut on the site of a village from the island's pre-Columbian past. It's open from 10 A.M. to 5 P.M daily.

MANDEVILLE

Welcome to "alpine" Jamaica, 2,000 feet above the sea. Mandeville, population 13,600, is a wonderful change of pace. Noted for its soft, cool climate and as the island's "most English" city, it's also within easy striking distance of uncrowded, secluded south-coast beaches. Seventy-two miles from either Montego Bay or Ocho Rios, 64 miles from Kingston, discover Mandeville now, before the crowd.

LODGING

The Astra (962–3265), 62 Ward Avenue, Mandeville, is a pleasant, family-run inn in a residential area. What this hostelry lacks in resort-style amenities, it more than makes up for in friendliness and a willingness to please. More to the point, here's where to find Diana McIntyre-Pike, the enthusiastic hostess and Mandeville's biggest booster; if she doesn't have time to show you around town herself, she'll point you in all the right directions.

There is a 24-hour visitor information center here (the only one in town), as well as a pool, sauna, a restaurant that serves up satisfying, homey Jamaican cuisine, and the popular Revival Pub. Horseback riding, golf, tennis, and excursions to local sights or Treasure Beach on the south coast can be arranged. If you book under the Modified American Plan (breakfast and dinner included), you can sample several area restaurants in addition to the Astra kitchen.

The inn's rooms range from about $55 to $90 per night double, and some have kitchenettes. A package that includes dinner starts at about $75 per night.

EXPLORING

Crisp, clear air, mountain scenery, and the pleasures of the great outdoors are the touring lures in Mandeville and its environs. Temperatures hover in the 60s in winter, in the 70s in summer. This is the garden and citrus center of the island, and the Jamaica Horticultural Society's show each summer is a microcosm of the best the island has to offer.

The town itself is orderly—you'll encounter no slums here, unlike elsewhere on the island—and has a tradition of wealth, thanks to its prominence as a bauxite-producing center. Many homes in the area are grand and imposing by anyone's standard. That certainly would describe the eight-sided mansion at 41 Manchester Road built by Cecil Charlton, a mayor of Mandeville for two decades—an indoor pool in the living room is connected to the outdoor swimming pool by an underground tunnel. Your hotel can make touring arrangements, except Wednesdays and Saturdays; no charge, but donations will go to local charity.

Mandeville's epicenter is the traditional town green, where you'll find a Georgian courthouse and a pretty parish church of native stone. But for the best view of the town and the surrounding countryside, make for the 150-year-old former hotel that is now **Bill Laurie's Steak House** (962–3116) in Bloomfield Gardens. A collection of antique cars sits out front, the restaurant itself reeks of history, and the panoramic view is unbeatable. Best time for photos is around 9 A.M.

Not far from the Hotel Astra, **Marshall's Pen** is a quarter-century-old great house on 300 acres of rolling countryside. An ideal setting for bird watchers, hikers, and lovers of high-country serenity, the antique-filled house is a private residence that can be toured on weekdays for about $5. Make arrangements through the Astra.

Northeast of town, where Routes B4, B5, and B6 converge, is Shooter's Hill. Alcan, the Canadian Aluminum Corporation, has its **Kirkvine Works** (962–3141) nearby—look for the red bauxite "lake" at the foot of the hill. Weekday tours can usually be arranged with a day's notice. Atop the hill is the tomb of the man who once owned this piece of real estate, Alexander Woodburn Heron; the Blue Mountain Peak, 60 miles distant, can be seen from this vantage point on clear days.

But to gourmet-shop devotees the most important stop at Shooter's Hill is the **Pickapeppa Factory** (962–2928), home to the famed piquant sauce that is sold worldwide; call ahead to see if a tour can be arranged.

Two more factory tours of note: The **High Mountain Coffee Factory** (962–4211) in the nearby town of Williamsfield, where Jamaica's exalted beans (including the renowned Blue Mountain) are processed and packed, can be toured weekdays by prior arrangement by phone or through your hotel. The same is true for the **Pioneer Chocolate Company** (962–4216), also in Williamsfield.

Sports—Sun & Fun

This is why you choose sunny Jamaica over, say, the Yukon—right? The sun. The sea. The sun. The golf. The sun. The tennis. The sun. And so on.

The great outdoors in the Caribbean—it doesn't get much better than this. We've hunted up the most fun you can have in the sun, and arranged it all alphabetically by category for easy reference. Spectator sports are covered at the end of the chapter. All prices listed are in U.S. currency.

BEST BEACHES

If "life is a beach," as the bumper sticker seen often back in the U.S.A. proclaims, then Jamaica is really *living*. We're talking about 200 miles of fine, soft, white sand, from cozy secluded cove to stretches that extend past the horizon.

Unless you're staying in Kingston—which is on the water but not on a beach—or in Mandeville—in the hilly interior—chances are that your hotel will either have its own private patch of sand, or access to one. Still, whether it's for privacy or a party scene or a place to broil *au naturel*, there are beaches in Jamaica definitely worth seeking out.

In general, the island's best beaches are on the north shore. And, in peak season, these are also the most likely to resemble Fort Lauderdale on spring break—especially around the most popular resorts of Montego Bay and Ocho Rios. Of the public beaches, most celebrated by far is **Doctor's Cave Beach** in Montego Bay. Popular with Jamaicans and visitors alike, this famed five-acre stretch of sugary sand has been the subject of countless travel articles and brochures over the years, all of which have contributed to its present status as the island's No. 1 sunning scene. Changing rooms are available. Vendors roam its length, and there is no lack of snacking opportunities nearby.

Doctor's Cave's overflow often heads just up the coast, to smaller **Cornwall Beach.** There's plenty of action here, too, as well as innumerable chances to find food and drink nearby. To the south, on the bay and very near the center of town, **Walter Fletcher Beach** offers another option: the protection of the bay affords unusually fine swimming.

In Ocho Rios, the "happening" beach is **Mallard's,** with the Sheraton and Americana hotels, as well as shops, bars, and restaurants galore, close at hand. But **Turtle Beach** to the south along the bay is public sand that is enjoyed by both islanders and tourists.

Other North-Coast public beaches worth tanning time include **Puerto Seco** at Discovery Bay; **San San** and **Boston Beach** (*the* place for "jerk pork") in Port Antonio. Ah, but for Jamaica's ultimate in unspoiled beach, head for the seven-mile-long strip of white sand at **Negril.** Especially at its northern end, you're likely to have plenty of breathing room.

Looking for uncrowded *and* undiscovered? Jamaica's south shore is little known to tourists, but that's for no reason other than the fact that it has yet to be developed to attract them. At these beaches you're only likely to encounter Jamaicans, and that alone makes them interesting and special. **Bluefields Beach,** near Savanna-la-Mar south of Negril along the coast, is quiet, and **Crane Beach** at Black River is both serene and scenic. It's another 20 miles along the coast (or about an hour's drive down from Mandeville) to **Treasure Beach,** the best beach on the south shore.

Kingstonians sometimes make the trek some 32 miles east to **Lyssons Beach** in Morant Bay, but favor other choices closer to home. Chief among these are the black-sand beaches of **Fort Clarence** in the Hellshire Hills area southwest of the city, which offer both changing facilities and frequent entertainment, including reggae; and the even better **Naggo Head** beyond, where rich and poor coexist in *irie* harmony. Another best bet: For a small, negotiable fee, you can hire a boat at the marina of Morgan's Harbour near Port Royal to ferry you to nearby **Lime Cay,** an island just beyond Kingston Harbour, for several hours of picnicking, sunning, and swimming.

Finally, back to Negril, the island's mecca for the uninhibited. Although Jamaicans themselves are rather reserved when it comes to nudity, it's commonplace at **Negril Beach** for visiting female sun worshippers to go topless. At the Hedonism II resort here, two beaches are reserved for nude sunbathing. Take-it-all-off tanning is also permitted at the private beaches of **Sandals** in Montego Bay, **Jamaica Jamaica** at Runaway Bay, and **Couples** in Ocho Rios.

BOATING

Many resorts offer small sailboats—Sunfish and Sailfish—for use free of charge by their guests; others charge roughly $10 an hour. Chartering larger craft for cruising or sailing is easy, except for bare-bottom charters, which are harder but not impossible to find. Contact one of the following: in the Kingston area, the **Royal Jamaica Yacht Club** (928–6685) or **Morgan's Harbour**

Marina (924–8464), which also berths visiting yachts; in MoBay, the **Montego Bay Yacht Club** (952–3028).

Water Sports Enterprises (953–2502) in Ocho Rios offers yacht excursions to Dunn's River Falls for about $15 per person, including drinks and dancing on the beach. From the harbor at Port Antonio, the catamaran *Lady Jamaica* cruises for an hour or so at about $5 per person; there's a longer sail that includes drinks and a snack for $10. Make reservations through your hotel.

CAMPING, CLIMBING, AND HIKING

The **Jamaica Alternative Tourism, Camping & Hiking Association** (JACHA), c/o Arthur's Golden Sunset Restaurant (957–4241), Norman Manley Boulevard, Negril, sets up camping and guest-house accommodations, as well as backpacking, biking, climbing, hiking, and river-canoeing trips.

Ever tried waterfall climbing? The most popular, but not the most challenging, hike in Jamaica is the 600-foot climb to the top of Dunn's River Falls near Ocho Rios. It's a wet adventure best done in a bathing suit; changing facilities are provided, and the climb costs about 50 cents per person, plus a guide (optional) to point out the slippery spots and snap your photo. The Nonsuch Caves south of Port Antonio offer both amateur and more serious adventurers interesting fossils, coral, and relics of a long-gone Arawak Indian settlement.

Hiking possibilities abound in the hills above the north-shore coastline, in the environs of Mandeville, and in the Blue Mountains in the southeastern part of the island. Serious climbers who wish to scale all or part of the 7,402-foot Blue Mountain Peak should contact the Jamaica Tourist Board (929–9200) for info on the series of mountain camps maintained by government foresters.

CYCLING

What better way to explore and enjoy the Jamaican coastline? Bicycles are loaned out by many hotels, and in Montego Bay, Ocho Rios, and Negril bike rentals are easy to find near the beaches and inexpensive—about $8 a day. A ride to Dunn's River Falls or Fern Gully in the Ocho Rios area, to Rose Hall near Montego Bay, or along the seven-mile strip of Negril beach is a particularly fine pedal.

Less exercise but more exhilarating is to make the trip on a moped, motor scooter, or small motorcycle. Mopeds and scooters are available through many hotels and some rental agencies at $15 or more per day. **Stony Hill Castle Ltd Bike Rentals** has locations in Montego Bay (953–2292), Ocho Rios (974–2681), and Negril (957–4460) and rents Honda 185 Trail bikes and CM200 Twin Stars at $38 a day; a Honda C50 Scooter is $18 per day. There are three-day and weekly rates as well; gasoline is extra. A deposit (or credit-card voucher) is required, and so is a valid driver's license.

FISHING

You've come to the right place. The freshwater catch from the island's rivers can be abundant, and the deep-sea bounty is often downright spectacular. No license is needed to try either.

Finny river dwellers include: drummer, mullet, snook, and tarpon. If you want a go at them, remember to bring your own tackle. Or, if you go river rafting on the Martha Brae River near Falmouth or the Rio Grande in Port Antonio, the raftsman will give you a baited line to dangle out.

Salt-water charters are most easily booked through your hotel, though a harborside stroll might land a better price, if your luck is good and the captain wants your business. Figure on about $450 for a full day, $225 for a half day, which includes boat, crew, tackle, and bait; some boats will take you aboard on a shared charter at around $75 a day, $55 a half day.

Port Antonio, especially, is known for some of the best deep-sea fishing in the Caribbean, but charters are also popular from Kingston, Ocho Rios, and, to a lesser extent, Negril. Blue and white marlin are the main attractions, and late summer and early winter are the best times to bait your hooks. Other challenging possibilities: barracuda, bonita, dolphin (*not* the Flipper kind), kingfish, sailfish, tuna (Allison and yellowfin), wahoo.

Spearfishing, legal along the reefs, can produce any number of species, including grouper, jack, mackerel, snapper, and tarpon. Bring your own gear.

GOLF

As you would expect of a nation with links to Great Britain (pardon the pun), golf is almost a religion here, with courses, pros, caddies, and greenskeepers to match any in the Caribbean. Greens fees in winter range from about $10 to $17 for 18 holes. And, unlike back home, it's usually cheaper—and certainly more instructive—to hire a caddy than to rent a cart; the former asks about $10 or less for 18 holes, the latter can cost upward of $25. For the fun of it, play at least a round or two with the smaller British ball and gloat over the extra distance in your drives.

In toto the island boasts nine courses, all with challenging holes and breathtaking vistas. Four of these are near Montego Bay. Though all are on hotel grounds, you don't have to be a guest to play. Unless otherwise specified, all have carts, caddies, and clubs for hire.

Tryall (952–5110), at the first-class resort of the same name, is a PGA Tour approved course with gorgeous links parallel to the sea. **Ironshore Golf Club** (953–2800) is characterized by beautifully kept fairways, lush greens, and the odd lake here and there. **Half Moon**

(953–2280) is part of the ultra-plush resort complex of the same name, and this dandy 18-holer was designed by Robert Trent Jones. Last but definitely not least is what *Golf Digest* termed "the most remarkable combination of highland, linksland, and crazy golf": **Wyndham Rose Hall** (933–2650).

A package called "Jamaica Championship Golf" offers visitors a round of golf each on the Tryall, Half Moon, and Wyndham Rose Hall courses for a single greens fee of $75. Caddies, carts, and club rentals are additional. The package can be booked through travel agents or by contacting the Jamaica Tourist Board.

In Ocho Rios, **Upton Golf Club** (974–2528) is nestled into the rolling countryside above town. It's worth playing the first nine for the tenth, with its sweeping panorama of the Caribbean. A few miles east along the coast, **Runaway Bay Golf Club** (973–2561) was laid out by James Harris, a British naval commander and golfing purist; it's a thinking golfer's course.

Manchester Club (962–2403) in Mandeville is the island's oldest course. Though it has only nine greens, its 18 tees allow each green to double up, as it were. Lush and green at more than 2,000 feet above sea level and the vistas are especially fine. No carts, but caddies and clubs are on hand.

In Kingston, tricky **Caymanas Golf Club** (926–8144) is home to the annual Jamaica Open. No carts, but caddies and a limited supply of clubs await. In a hilly northern suburb, **Constant Spring** (924–1610) is short, tight, and challenging. No carts, but caddies and clubs are available.

HORSEBACK RIDING

A sense of Jamaica's past comes on horseback, since many of the best riding opportunities are on historic plantations or ranches. Or, in the case of **Chukka Cove Farms** (972–2506) on the former Llandovery estate west of Ocho Rios, there's an echo of the island's colonial tie to Great Britain. Polo instruction, anyone? How about jumping and dressage? This is one of the finest equestrian centers in the West Indies, and it leads picnic, trail, and moonlight rides at about $10 an hour per person.

Guided rides elsewhere in Ocho Rios are at **Prospect Estates** (974–2058); in Montego Bay, **Good Hope Plantation** (954–2289) and **White Witch Stables** (953–2746); and in Negril, **Hedonism II** (957–4200). In Port Antonio, the 2,000-acre ranch owned by film star Errol Flynn's widow can usually accommodate would-be trail riders; check with your hotel. At any of the above, the going rate is roughly $10 an hour.

PARASAILING

Ride that giant kite tethered to a speeding power boat—up, up, you climb until you are like a huge, multicolored bird against the deep blue sky! This parasailing —now a craze—is undeniably a thrill, and one you can experience in Negril, Montego Bay, and Ocho Rios. Figure on about $15 for a 25-minute soar. Ask at your hotel where to find the local parasailing action.

RIVER RAFTING

Swashbuckling Errol Flynn, the Forties film star, is said to have invented this only-in-Jamaica adventure when he decided that the long, thin bamboo rafts used by the islanders to transport bananas could ferry passengers equally as well. Today raftsmen guide two passengers at a time through winding tropical countryside, ending finally at the river's mouth; minirapids even add a little excitement to the journey.

The best, and original, rafting is on the Rio Grande, starting at Berrydale south of Port Antonio; the leisurely three-hour trip to the sea costs about $45 per raft. A shorter trip down the Martha Brae River starts south of Falmouth (west of MoBay) and costs about $35 for two. Your hotel can make reservations.

SCUBA AND SNORKELING

Jamaica underwater is, if anything, more fascinating than it is above-sea-level. The clear, warm waters of the Caribbean invite snorkelers and divers to explore the rainbow-hued coral reefs and volcanic shoals—and they are rewarded by brightly colored fish and gently swaying sea flora. At depths of 200 yards or more, divers can hunt centuries-old shipwrecks and photograph larger, even more dramatic marine life.

Almost every area on the north shore harbors its own sea scenery. Kingston harbor, because of its long history of ocean-crossing traffic and pirate past, is a favorite among divers.

Several hotels, especially the all-inclusives, offer snorkel gear, as well as scuba instruction and a free tank a day as part of the package. To rent scuba gear or participate in guided scuba trips from a dive shop, you must show a certification card—unless you sign up for an instruction course.

A one-tank scuba trip costs about $30, with a certified diving instructor and all equipment; snorkel trips run roughly $10. Scuba instruction—three hours in a pool and a one-tank dive in open water—costs $50 or more.

Among reputable dive shops that rent scuba and snorkel gear and lead guided trips are: In Montego Bay, **Seaworld** at the Rose Hall Beach Hotel (953–2250) and Cariblue Beach (953–2180); and **Poseidon Nimrod Divers** (952–3624). In the Ocho Rios area, **Island Dive Shop** (972–2519), **Sea and Dive Jamaica** (972–2162), and **Water Sports Enterprises** (974–2185). In Negril, **Aqua Nova** (957–4323), **Hedonism II Water Sports** (957–4200) and **Negril Scuba Center** (957–4323). In Port Antonio, **Huntress Marine** (993–3318).

SURF'S UP!

Though not noted for the power of its surf, Jamaica isn't without its tubular thrills. Head for Boston Bay, east of Port Antonio on the north shore, where the waves are as near to perfect as anywhere on the island.

TENNIS

This is another game Jamaicans take seriously. They play early in the morning or on night-lit courts to avoid the sizzle of the Caribbean sun—and you should do likewise unless you are in exceptional shape or the thermometer registers in the mid-70s or lower. Heat and humidity can take a quick toll on the unwary.

The good news: Lots of courts—more than 130 across the island, with the greatest concentration in MoBay and Ocho Rios. Nearly every major hotel has at least one, and nonguests can usually play for a court fee of about $7 an hour; guests play for free. Several resorts also have resident pros and clubhouses.

A parting shot of advice: Bring an extra can or two of tennis balls if you intend to play often. Like many imported items, they're expensive here.

WATER-SKIING

Yet another wet 'n' wild activity that is offered free to guests at many hotels. Otherwise the going rate is about $1 a minute. The Blue Lagoon in Port Antonio and Doctor's Cave Beach in Montego Bay are two popular places to slice across the water on skis.

Jet skiing is another speedy alternative. Skis can be

rented—about $15 for half an hour—at Cornwall Beach in MoBay and Turtle Beach in Ocho Rios.

WINDSURFING

Devotees of windsurfing—it's also called sailboard-ing—can catch the wind in their sails at any number of hotel beaches, where this sport is offered as part of the activities program. Instruction is also commonly avail-able. It's a great spectator sport, too, watching the ex-perts twist and turn and perform incredible acrobatics.

SPECTATOR SPORTS

Do you like to watch? When it comes to organized sport, things are veddy British here. Cricket is the nation-al mania, and international matches—"tests"—are played from January through August in Sabina Park, Kingston. Soccer—it's called football here—runs a close second. The season begins in the fall and runs through the winter; check the *Daily Gleaner* for info about matches, or ask at your hotel or the nearest Jamaica Tourist Bu-reau office.

And then there's polo. This sport of kings is played on Saturdays throughout the year at Drax Hall, five miles west of Ocho Rios; and on Thursdays and Sundays at Caymanas Park, in a western suburb of Kingston.

Restaurants

Adapting Jamaica's motto slightly, it becomes: "Out of many, one cuisine." Indeed, from a cultural stew begun centuries ago that has come to include Arawak Indian, Spanish, African, English, East Indian, Chinese, Syrian, and more, flavors have emerged that, while related to those found elsewhere in the Caribbean and the world, are at the same time distinctly Jamaican.

While there is no lack of more familiar fare—including Continental, Italian, and Chinese cuisine, broiled fresh seafood, even, yes, fast-food burgers and fried chicken—don't pass up the opportunity to eat as the Jamaicans do. Especially if you enjoy food on the spicy side, you will discover much to love here.

Soups, in particular, are akin to a folk art. Pepperpot is thick and meaty and, despite its name, will warm you without setting you afire; it's made from salt pork, beef, okra, coconut milk, and callaloo, a local leafy vegetable. Other delights include fish "tea," conch soup (made from the mullosk whose beautiful shell is sold to tourists along the north shore), red pea, and pumpkin.

Ackee and saltfish are part of every traditional Jamaican breakfast (but, as the national dish, is also served at other times)—it's cod, an exotic fruit brought to the island by the notorious Captain Bligh that tastes remarkably like scrambled eggs when baked, onions, and slices of hot peppers. An acquired taste for many, but worth a try.

Curries, hot and flavorful, are common. Curried goat is a popular main dish; have it with the excellent Jamaican mango chutney. Other local favorites that shouldn't be missed: roast suckling pig, rice and peas (kidney beans, actually, and cooked in coconut milk), stamp and go (spicy cod fritters), and akcra cakes (vegetable fritters). Patties—tasty pastries filled with ground beef, breadcrumbs, onion, and lively seasonings—are everywhere in Jamaica, the national snack or lunch.

A few words about jerk pork, jerk chicken, and jerk fish. They're all sensational, if you like barbecue. "Jerk" is derived from a Spanish word of Indian origin, and means to prepare pork (the only *authentic* jerked meat, though chicken and fish are equally delicious) in the manner of the Quechua Indians of South America. The method of slow cooking over a fire of green pimento wood was thought to have been learned by the Arawaks of Jamaica, passed to the Maroons—the freed slaves of the Spanish colonialists—then adopted by the rest of the island by the 19th century. Today you'll find roadside purveyors of this special treat throughout the island, especially along the North Coast, but devotees insist the very best is to be found along the beach at Boston Bay, east of Port Antonio.

Need something cooling after the tang of jerk pork or a patty? Jamaican fruit is excellent, from the familiar banana, coconut, orange, and pineapple to the more exotic guava, mango, passion fruit, pawpaw (papaya), rose apples, and soursop. From February to April, in the star-apple season, look for a salad dish called "matrimony," a sensuous marriage of star apples, either green-skinned or purple, oranges, milk, nutmeg, and sugar. Native fruits also make delectable tarts and ice creams.

Thirsty? Blue Mountain coffee is revered by gourmands everywhere, and Jamaican rum is some of the world's finest. Myers and Appleton rums, white or dark, have a longstanding rivalry as the island's best. So-called "overproof" rum, available under various labels, is favored by many locals; it has a taste all its own, but is extremely potent.

Tia Maria, the coffee liqueur, is also a native product, as is the lesser-known Rumona, a rum cordial. Sangster's Old Jamaica liqueurs come in five varieties (and lovely ceramic bottles), including Blue Mountain Coffee and Orantique, a unique hybrid of orange and tangerine.

Red Stripe beer, the island brew, is likewise excellent. Oh, and not only is Jamaican water perfectly fine to drink, it tastes good.

Not perfectly fine to drink: mushroom tea. Especially in Negril, you'll come across places that sell this dangerous concoction made from psylicybin, or "magic," mushrooms. It may produce hallucinations. It may make you very sick to your stomach.

Dining out in Jamaica is not typically a dressy affair—only those establishments in the upscale resorts of the North Coast and the better restaurants of Kingston require that men wear a jacket and tie to dinner—but except for the most laid-back, beachside eatery, bare feet and bikinis aren't acceptable either.

The establishments listed below offer some of Jamaica's very finest eating. Arranged by location, they accept all major credit cards unless otherwise noted. Remember that many restaurants add a 10 percent gratuity to the check. Prices quoted are in U.S. currency.

NEGRIL

This is a place of serendipity. Some of the best eating you find here will be the lucky discovery, the tiny hole-in-wall, the thatched-roof snack bar, the Rastaman barbecuing chicken by the roadside. In this category falls **Chicken Lavish** (no phone) on the lighthouse road south of town. Casual to the max, this little place's freshly caught fish or its terrific chicken, plus salad and dessert, will set you back less than $10.

But there are the well-known, even famous, places,

too. Chief among these is **Rick's Cafe** (957–4335), also on the lighthouse road. They say Rick's is perched on the westernmost promontory in Jamaica; it certainly has no peers when it comes to sunset watching . . . or watching the sunset watchers. It's *the* meet 'n' greet spot in Negril. Used to be it was quite a trek to get to Rick's, but now the road is paved, and the tour buses make the trip regularly. But you can still dive off the craggy rocks into the incredibly blue-green sea below.

You order at the blackboard before being seated on the open-air terrace overlooking the sea below. Breakfast or brunch might be a lobster omelet, or smoked marlin and cream cheese on a toasted bagel (most choices are between $4 to $8). Dinner could range from a mixed grill of fresh fish ($12) to steamed shrimp with lime (about $22) or there are more moderate entrees in the $7 neighborhood. Open daily from 9:30 A.M. to 11 P.M. No credit cards.

"Informal but elegant" is the dress code at the **Charela Inn** (957–4277), less than a mile north of town on Norman Manley Boulevard—and that about sums up the mood. Five-course dinners combining French and Jamaican cuisine are served with down-home aplomb here—entrees like lobster Creole and stuffed baked crab —on the outdoor patio by the beach or in the classy indoor dining room. About $18 per person before drinks. The patio is perfect for a leisurely breakfast or lunch. Open daily from 8 A.M. to 10 P.M.

MONTEGO BAY

The **Calabash** (952–3891), 5 Queen's Drive, has both a superb view of the bay below and some of the finest seafood and Jamaican cooking in MoBay. Look for the blue awning marking the entrance in the Winged Victory Hotel. A casual dinner house, the Calabash's tasty specialty is a combo of baked crabmeat, lobster, shrimp, and white fish in a blue-cheese-and-brandy sauce. Also recommended: spicey pork. And if tropical drinks appeal, don't miss their "house" mix of rum, liqueurs, and juices. The cost is about $20 per person, without drinks or wine. Open 6 to 9:30 P.M. daily.

A few steps down Queen's Drive stands a stately colonial mansion turned restaurant that has become a place to be seen as much as a place to dine. **The Diplomat** (952–3353) affords an equally stunning view of the ultramarine sea. Steaks, fresh seafood, and international fare—but it's the ambience and setting that makes it worth $25 or more per diner. Open for dinner daily, except Sunday. It's popular, so reservations are a good idea.

Less fancy, less expensive, but no less popular is **The Front Porch** (952–2854), 39 Gloucester Avenue, not far from Doctor's Cave Beach. It's in a porchlike section of the Wexford Hotel (which actually fronts a small street off Gloucester called Corniche Court), and it's the real thing, Jamaica-style. Huge portions of curried goat, chicken fricassee, fresh fish as well as baked-on-premises cakes and pies. And a steal—$10 per person should do it for dinner. Open daily for breakfast, lunch, and dinner. American Express only.

Across Gloucester Avenue from the Coral Cliff Hotel and right at water's edge is a jewel of a place called **Marguerite's by the Sea** (952–4777). Here's how much they aim to please: They'll provide free transportation to and from most hotels. Once here, choose between the seaside terrace or the attractive indoor dining room. Either way, the service is professional, and the food reliably good to excellent. Try the lobster sauté flamed with brandy or the "daily Caribbean catch" steamed in coconut milk. About $25 per person for dinner, and worth it. Open for dinner daily.

Among the many possibilities along action-packed Kent Avenue, we'd suggest the **Cornwall Beach** (no phone) as a quick, dependable lunch stop. It's extremely casual and open to cooling sea breezes. The burgers are good, but so are the few Jamaican dishes offered. Your tab should run in the $5 range.

In the thick of historic MoBay, the **Town House** (952–2660), 16 Church Street, is across from the old Parish Church and is older. The brick structure was built in 1765, a decade before the church. A host of visiting celebs, including Paul McCartney, Dustin Hoffman, and the Duke of Marlborough, have broken bread here over the years. The fare is a pleasing assortment of Jamaican (smoked marlin, pumpkin soup), Continental (red snapper mornay), American (steak, spare ribs), and fresh seafood (steamed yellow tail, broiled lobster). Entrees range from $9 to $18. Open for lunch and dinner; dinner only Sundays. Free pick-up service from your hotel.

On a hill above town, the **Richmond Hill** (952–3859) is a wonderfully romantic great house built in the 1700s that has been converted to a small inn and restaurant. The views are delightful, especially at night, as you dine by candlelight on an open-air terrace near the pool. The steaks and lobster are first-rate, but chicken lovers will go for the house preparation of boneless breasts stuffed with spinach and topped with a cream sauce. Dinner entrees start at $18; at lunch, $10 and up. Open daily. There's entertainment at night, as well as courtesy round-trip transportation.

Two special splurges at MoBay-area resorts: The first, at **Tryall Golf and Beach Club** (952–5110), a dozen miles west of town on the coast highway, Route A1. On a terrace of the superb great house that commands the hillside, you dine under the stars—anything from a thick steak to the chef's own Jamaica-style paella—drink from the extensive wine list, then cap the evening off with dancing and entertainment. Monday nights see a vast seafood buffet, Fridays, a beach barbecue and native floor show. Figure $25 or more per person, without drinks or wine. Jackets required for gentlemen; reservations a must. Dinner nightly from November through mid-May only.

The other special evening awaits at the **Club House Grill** (953–2228) of the swank Half Moon Club, seven miles east of town on Route A1. There's a picturesque waterwheel as you enter, and dining is on the candlelit patio. The kitchen can be imaginative—as in the ackee tart appetizer—but as the name implies, the emphasis here is on simply but beautifully prepared steaks, roast beef, chops, lobster, and other fresh sea bounty. Entrees range from $8 to $22. Dress is informal (no shorts) at lunch, but gentlemen will feel more comfortable in jackets at dinner. Lunch and dinner are served daily; reservations are essential.

RUNAWAY BAY

If you're staying near Runaway Bay or are driving the North Coast between Montego Bay and Ocho Rios, consider this next find. In Brown's Town, about 10 miles south from the coast on Route B3, **Country Life** (975–2317) is a few tables covered by a thatched roof on a hilltop. Just below is a makeshift bird sanctuary that cages everything from chickens to a doctor's bird (the national bird). Nothing fancy about this place, but if you want to sample real Jamaican cooking at its finest in an out-of-the-way, real-life setting, you've arrived. Fish "tea," curried goat, ackee and saltfish, rice and peas, deep-fried Johnny cakes, boiled green bananas with rundown sauce all range from $5 to $15 an eater. Open daily for lunch and dinner, but it might be a good idea to phone Mrs. Melton, the proprietress, to let her know you're coming.

OCHO RIOS

A moveable feast in Ocho would proceed along Main Street, and a great place to start is the **Almond Tree** (974–2813) on the seaside back patio of the Hibiscus Lodge (near the Catholic Church). Your visit should begin in the bar, where the "stools" are swinging chairs; actually, it may have to, because this is a busy place in high season, and even those with reservations often wait with an Almond Tree Delight—a house drink made of rums, cherry liqueur, strawberry, oranges and lime juices —or two. Dinner is best here, with its candlelit views of the Caribbean and an extensive menu that includes fondue bourguinonne, steak Diane, and crabmeat Milanese. Expect to pay $18 or more per person before drinks. Open daily for lunch and dinner.

Good for an inexpensive breakfast, lunch, or drinks while watching the entertainment that begins nightly at 10 P.M. is the **Little Pub** (974–2324), on Main Street in the center of town. Dinner is also served here, but even with entrees under $6, well, you might get better value elsewhere. Open daily.

A short walk further on Main, near the roundabout and clock tower, the **Parkway** (974–2667) is short on atmosphere but long on good Jamaican fare, steaks, and lobster at prices that start at only $3. That's why it's crowded with local clientele. Come as you are from 8 A.M. to 11 P.M. No credit cards.

If you walk south from the roundabout (away from the sea) and right on DaCosta Drive, you'll spot what may be *the* hot spot in Ocho. It's called **The Ruins** (974–2442). Lovely public gardens are up the hill. A 40-foot-high waterfall cascades into the Turtle River here, and you cross into the dining area over a footbridge. The menu is extensive, but regulars know the Chinese cuisine is best—especially the "lotus lily lobster," stir-fried and gingery, and priced at about $22. Other entrees begin in the $12 range. Attire is dressy casual. Open for lunch daily, except Sunday; dinner daily. Reservations should be made in peak season.

About four miles east of the town center along coastal Route A1, **Casanova** (974–2353) in the Sans Souci Hotel is a magical place. Stylish, romantic, with views of the hotel's gardens, Casanova also boasts superb service and perhaps the most ambitious kitchen in the area. Specialties include marinated dolphin with mango relish, smoked marlin, exquisite preparations of lobster and fresh fish, plus homemade pasta and other Italian renditions. Figure about $25 per person without drinks or wine. Dress up a little (jackets not required), and make reservations. Open for lunch and dinner daily; closed in summer.

About half a mile further east, the **Kings Arms** (974–4233) on the open-air patio of Harmony Hall great house is good for everything from steak-and-kidney pie or fish and chips to lobster. Best of all, you can eat well for under $5. Open daily for lunch, snacks, and dinner.

Eight miles east of Ocho Rios, but worth the trip, is **Moxon's of Boscobel** (974–3234), the self-proclaimed "famous little place where the famous dine." (These famed patrons past include Alex Haley, Henry Kissinger, and Pierre Trudeau.) It's a cozy, candlelit place at water's edge that serves its own paté, lobster or steak in several guises, fresh fish, and homemade sweets. Entrees range from about $9.50 to $15.50. Jackets not required, "but elegance is"; so are reservations. Dinner daily.

PORT ANTONIO

The **Bonnie View Hotel** (993–2752) on Bonnie View Road above town has lovely views of the twin harbors, a pleasant afternoon tea, plus home-style Jamaican dinners at budget prices. Expect to be satisfied for $8 or less per person. Open daily for breakfast, lunch, and dinner. On the peninsula between the harbors, the gingerbready **DeMontevin Lodge** (993–2604), Musgrave and George streets, is a family-run place that will treat you like one of their own at dinnertime if you call a day ahead for reservations. The owner used to cook for Errol Flynn. About $15 or so per appetite.

Humble, homey fare is not your only choice, however. **Trident Villas and Hotel** (993–2602) offers one of the best dining experiences in Jamaica, if not in the Caribbean. The sterling gleams and the cut crystal shines in this intimate, elegant room as your seven-course meal, served by white-gloved waiters, begins. The menu changes daily—there is no choice of selections—but put yourself in the hands of Trident's capable chef. A sample meal: hearts of palm, red-pea soup, steamed lobster in tarragon butter, avocado vinaigrette, tournedos of beef with potato and callaloo, champagne sherbet, coffee with Tia Maria.

This prix-fixe feast costs about $40 per person, not including wine. Open daily for dinner; reservations should be made by 5 P.M. Jacket and tie are required for men in winter season, jacket only at other times.

A short distance east of Trident is the much more modest **Castle Cove** (no phone). It's a thatched-roof affair near water's edge that couldn't be friendlier. The food they serve couldn't be better, or more reasonably priced. Steamed butterfish with ample amounts of well-seasoned rice and peas, plus yams goes for under $5. No credit cards.

The **Blue Lagoon** (993–2495) is a bar with a few tables at the edge of this famed local landmark. The food offerings are limited, but tasty; ask for the barbecued chicken (under $5). Open daily for lunch and dinner.

Boston Bay, just beyond, is *the* place for jerk pork. Jerk chicken and jerk fish are fine, too. Pick out a beach-side vendor and join the legion of "jerk lovers."

KINGSTON

As you would expect of Jamaica's capital and largest metropolitan area, Kingston offers the island's most varied restaurant scene, including such ethnic fare as Chinese, Indian, German, Korean, Mexican, and Middle Eastern.

Probably the most famous—and certainly the most romantic—dining spot locally is a half-hour drive out of town. The **Blue Mountain Inn** (927–7400) on the Gordon Town Road (Route B1), a great house built in 1754 on a coffee plantation, sits on the banks of the Hope River in the mountains, surrounded by dense vegetation. Cocktails are served out on the terrace, and dinner follows in the elegant, candle-lit dining room inside.

The menu is Continental with the occasional Jamaican accent, as in the ackee quiche. Pork prepared with cognac and sour cream, as well as scallops of lobster sauteed with shallots, are prized by many, although it is only fair to say that the magnificent surroundings overshadow the kitchen on some nights. The wine list is superior, perhaps best on the island, with imported vintages starting at about $15. Figure on about $20 per person for dinner, not including drinks or wine.

Jackets and ties are required for gentlemen, and ladies should be prepared for the cool of the mountain night on the terrace. The Blue Mountain is open for dinner only, from 7:30 to 9:30 P.M., except Sunday. Reservations are a must.

If you don't have a rental car, a limousine service operates from the Courtleigh, Oceana, Jamaica Pegasus, and Terra Nova hotels; the round trip is about $5. Otherwise, taxi fare there and back will cost around twice that.

In the New Kingston area, the **Surrey Tavern** (926–3690) in the Jamaica Pegasus Hotel is an English-style pub that features a popular, reasonably priced luncheon buffet. On Friday and Saturday evenings (from 7:30 to 9:30 P.M.), sample the steak-and-kidney pie or other pub fare while listening to good live jazz. Lunch is served weekdays only.

Seventeen floors up, the elegant **Talk of the Town** (926–3690) offers both spectacular city views and a menu that is Continental and elaborate. Candlelight dining is extra special here. Try the complexity of flavors in the fillet of snapper with jumbo shrimps "Pierre le Grand." Open for lunch weekdays, dinner daily from 7 P.M.; reservations and jackets for men are suggested.

Nearby, in the Wyndham New Kingston, the panoramic rooftop vistas are just as stunning, the ambience as upscale, and the northern Italian fare is downright righteous at **Ristorante d'Amore** (926–5430). Recommended: *piccola marmitta di pesce dei Caraibi,* an array of Caribbean seafood simmered in a fish-and-vegetable stock and served on pasta. Musicians add the background soundtrack in the evenings. Plan on $25 or more per person, sans liquor. Open for lunch weekdays; dinner served daily. Jackets for men, reservations are a good idea.

Rumours (929–7904), 3 Dumfries Road, is a friendly, pub-like place with Jamaican country decor not far from the Wyndham and Pegasus. Sandwiches, burgers, and salads are served at lunch; at dinner, more ambitious items like stuffed lobster (about $9), or avocado and shrimp ($7); steaks and shish kebabs, too. Fridays from

5 to 7 P.M. there's a happy hour with free hors d'oeuvres and reduced prices. Open for lunch and dinner, Monday through Friday; dinner only on Saturday.

At Hope and Waterloo roads, **The Grog Shop** (926–3580) is on the back patio of the government-owned Devon House, facing a serene courtyard edged by attractive shops. The staff dresses in 19th-century garb, the traditional Jamaican cuisine is well prepared, and it's hard to imagine a more pleasing setting to shut out the big city beyond. You can grab a quick snack here like a crab cake (about $2), or opt for a full lunch or dinner at moderate prices. The full bar serves everything from ice-cold Red Stripes beer to exotic rum concoctions. Before or after, stroll across the way and try a scoop of soursop ice cream (about 50 cents) at **I Scream** or a plantain tart (40 cents) at **The Bread Basket.** Open for lunch and dinner daily, except Sunday; reservations advisable for dinner.

The **Terra Nova** (926–2211), 17 Waterloo Road, is a former private residence turned hotel and restaurant that's a hangout for Kingston swells and government types. The menu is Continental, and you can expect to pay $20 or more apiece at dinner. The fun here is the crowd, and the late-evening scene—the place is a hot dance spot and nightclub, as well. Open for breakfast, lunch, and dinner daily. Reservations are a good idea for dinner, and so are jackets for gentlemen.

Another hotel that draws crowds for its food is the hospitable **Mayfair** (926–1610), 4 West King's House Close, near the parklike grounds that surround the government buildings, King's House, and Jamaica House. Jim and Sybil Hughes are genial hosts of the popular poolside buffet (about $10 on Wednesday evenings) and Saturday night barbecues ($7 to $10) from 7:30 to 9 P.M. Reservations are strongly suggested.

In Port Royal across Kingston harbor, **Morgan's Harbour** (924–8464) serves breakfast, lunch, and dinner, as well as sandwiches and snacks. You can't beat the view—yachts bobbing in the marina only feet from your table, the harbor and skyline of Kingston beyond. You can't beat the relaxed, get-away-from-it-all ambience— nautical casual, like that of a shipshape boating club. And the kitchen? Make straight for the fresh seafood: Lobster cocktail is under $2, a whole grilled lobster is about $12. Open daily, except Sunday.

MANDEVILLE

Hotel Astra (962–3265), 62 Ward Avenue, serves breakfast, lunch, and dinner daily in a pleasant, informal setting. Nicely prepared international and Jamaican entrees, including lobster thermidor and fresh-fish specials, range from about $6.50 to $15.00. The Friday-night poolside barbecue is popular, as is the Sunday breakfast buffet. The hotel's **Revival Room Pub** also offers homemade pizza, burgers, and seafood salads.

If you have time for only one meal in Mandeville, make it at **Bill Laurie's Steak House** (962–3116) in Bloomfield Gardens. Set on a hilltop with spectacular views of the town and surrounding countryside, the restaurant is a 150-year-old hotel presided over by Mr. Laurie, an engaging Scotsman in his 70s who looks and acts like Central Casting found him to play the last holdover from colonial rule. His collection of antique autos is out front. Inside, the bar's walls are covered with auto-license plates and yellowed business cards from patrons the world over; a grand piano with candles resting on its top awaits the next sing-along. In short, you'd swear you had been transported back in time.

How's the food? Uncomplicated and cooked-to-order steaks, chops, and fresh fish. Figure on about $15 per person, without drinks. Open daily for lunch and dinner. No credit cards.

Nightlife

Jamaica's biggest spectacle is absolutely free and occurs nightly. Sunset, it's called. At places like Rick's Cafe in Negril, high on a cliff at the island's westernmost vantage point, the setting of Old Sol each day is a celebration marked by ahs of appreciation, rum drinks raised in toast, and the emergence of that good-times-seeking creature, the nocturnal party animal. He or she has come to the right island, for making merry into the wee hours is standard operating procedure in the major resort areas. And wherever you are, it all begins with a few moments' pause to bid farewell to the heat of day. And to welcome the night—be it cultured or crazy, cool or red hot.

Prices quoted for the following nightspots and events are in U.S. currency.

BARS, CABARETS, AND CLUBS

The island's bars, clubs, and cabarets give you the choice of soft, romantic background music, reverberating disco tunes, hypnotic reggae, or many steps in between.

Keep this in mind: Wherever there's a large resort hotel, you'll find a smorgasbord of nightlife—and lots of fellow lovers of the night—under one roof. The competition for your business is such that each hotel manager is constantly on the lookout for ways to get you happily through the night. This is especially so when the hotel is situated on the outskirts, beyond easy walking distance to anywhere else.

If you're in Montego Bay or Ocho Rios, the two most developed tourist havens, finding nighttime fun is as easy as strolling through the center of things and keeping an eye peeled and an ear cocked. If one place isn't quite your style, proceed to the next. In sprawling, confusing Kingston and in less raucous towns like Port Antonio, Mandeville, and Negril, some advance planning is required to keep your scouting time to a minimum and party time to the max.

Of course, of all there is to see and do in Jamaica, the night scene is the most changeable. Clubs come and go; the hot spot now is replaced by another in a few months' time. Here's our list of favorites . . .

NEGRIL

In Negril, apart from watching the sunset and its afterglow at the aforementioned **Rick's Cafe** (957–4335, on the lighthouse road south of town) reggae groups often hold forth there in the evenings. Go for the sunset and ask if anything's planned for later on. Open daily till 11 P.M.

Another possibility for reggae is the **Negril Tree House Club** (957–4287) on Norman Manley Boulevard along the beach. It gets going after 10 P.M. and cooks till the wee hours. Best to call ahead.

Gotta dance? Do it to both reggae and stateside sounds at one of the liveliest discos on the island—at **Hedonism II** (957–4200), Rutland Point, on the seven-mile beach. Opens at 11 P.M. nightly. A $35 package includes a meal and all drinks.

MONTEGO BAY

No doubt about it, Montego Bay is the party capital of Jamaica. The highlights: On the downtown beachfront hotel strip, the action is at **Fantasy Disco** in the Casa Montego Hotel (952–4150), 2 Kent Avenue. It's open from 10 P.M. to 3 A.M. nightly; cover charge of $17 includes drinks. For a more subdued evening, try the nightly piano bar at **Doctor's Cave Beach Hotel** (952–4355) on Gloucester Avenue near the famous white sand of the same name.

On Sunset Drive at the south end of the bay, off the picturesque inlet known as Montego Bay Freeport, the **Cave** disco is a solid hit at the Seawind Beach Resort (952–4874). Opens at 10 P.M. nightly; admission is $4.

On the coast Route A1 in the Rose Hall area, the club called **Witch's Hideaway** at Rose Hall Holiday Inn (953–2485) has withstood the test of time. It gets going at 9 P.M. every night, and there is no cover charge. Ditto for the **Jonkanoo Lounge** at the Wyndham Rose Hall Hotel (953–2650).

Newer, but hotter of late, is nearby **Disco Inferno** at Holiday Village (953–2113). For a cover of $3, you can start dancing at 9:30 P.M. nightly. On Mondays, Wednesdays, and Saturdays, come earlier for the lobster party. For $30, there's a buffet with lobster, chicken, shrimp, and more, an open bar from 7 to 11 P.M., live reggae, and dance contests.

OCHO RIOS

The Ruins (974–2442) on DaCosta Drive just south of the Ocho Rios roundabout is the town's foremost venue for meeting and greeting. With its spectacular mountain waterfall and lily ponds, the surroundings themselves are enough—but the bar serves an honest drink, too. The bar stays open to 10:30 P.M., and there's a steel band playing almost till closing.

The **Little Pub** (974–2324) in the heart of town has a nightly 10 P.M. show featuring calypso and dance music. Admission is $4. The disco action is best at **Silks** at the Shaw Park Beach (974–2552) on the coast Route A3 shortly before the White River bridge. It opens at 9 P.M. nightly; cover charge is $4. Another hot spot is **Maroons** at the Americana Hotel (974–2151) on Mallard's Beach. Opens at 10 P.M. nightly, with a $3 admission.

For danceable reggae in Ocho, the most established venue is **Footprints** in the Coconut Grove Shopping Center (974–2239).

PORT ANTONIO

In Port Antonio, **Fern Hill** (993–3223) is on a local hill of the same name and keeps the neighborhood lively upon occasion with a live reggae show at 9:30 P.M. This is a members-only club, but a phone call can usually set up admittance. If you want to rub shoulders with the *real* Jamaica, seek out **Blue Jays, Centre Point, Castle Cove,** or the **First & Last Club**—all local nightspots. None has a phone. Ask at your hotel for directions.

KINGSTON

In Kingston, the Jamaica Pegasus Hotel (926–3690) at 81 Knutsford Boulevard houses two admirable nightspots. The **Surrey Tavern** (926–3690), a friendly English-style pub by day, turns into the hottest place to hear live jazz in the capital several nights a week. The sounds start around 8:30 P.M. Call ahead to make sure tonight's the night. Up on the 17th floor, at **Talk of the Town,** there's always the spectacular view of the city and often a good combo or singer after 8 P.M.

At the nearby Wyndham New Kingston (926–5430), 77 Knutsford Boulevard, the **Jonkanoo Lounge** features slick nightclub-type acts with an 11 P.M. showtime and a cover charge of about $5.

The **Atlantis Night Club** (929–4387), 69 Knutsford Boulevard, describes itself as "the Jamaican way to play." This disco opens at 11 P.M. Thursday through Saturday; admission is $5. Another local favorite in the New Kingston area on Thursdays through Saturday is the **Epiphany** disco (929–1130), 1 St. Lucia Avenue. Cover charge is $5.

The **Terra Nova Hotel** (926–2211), 17 Waterloo Road, is the place where you may see a government minister dancing with, presumably, his wife. This former private residence is a hangout for Kingston society and high bureaucrats. The fun begins after 9 P.M. **Mingles,** the nightspot at the Courtleigh Hotel (926–8174), 31 Trafalgar Road, is a hit with both visiting and resident Brits. Open nightly; admission is $5.

MANDEVILLE

Bill Laurie's Steak House (962–3116) in Mandeville's Bloomfield Gardens is just the place to while away an evening, or two or three. . . . This hilltop aerie affords great views, and the bar couldn't be cozier or more atmospheric with its dark wood, antique auto license plates, and yellowed business cards from former patrons tacked to every available space. The grand piano sits nearby, and no one will laugh if you sit down to play. On a good night the singing and dancing last into the morning hours. Open daily.

The **Revival Room Pub** in the Hotel Astra (962–3265), 62 Ward Avenue, is another convivial spot frequented by both locals and visitors to this tidy, alpinelike city. The Mandeville visitor information center is located at the hotel, and so this is a good place to begin any tour of the environs, day or night. The center is open 24 hours. The pub is open daily.

To check out the local disco scene—remember, this is not really a tourist town—ask for directions to **Planet** or **Tracks,** both in Mandeville Plaza; **Intime** in Willogate Shopping Center; or **Zee-X** in Caledonia Plaza. None has a phone, and not all may be open nightly.

BOONOONOONOOS

In local patois, the word means as good as it gets, something extraordinary. At all the larger resort hotels, there's at least one *boonoonoonoos* event weekly, usually a torchlit-poolside or beachfront buffet or barbecue, accompanied by strolling calypso musicians or a steel band and then capped off with a show—double-jointed limbo dancers, barefooted walkers on live coals, and the like. It's all worth seeing, at least once.

But the *boonoonoonoos* have only just begun. In Montego Bay, the **Cornwall Beach Party** gets underway each Friday at 7 P.M. For about $22 per person, there's an open rum bar, Jamaican music, a buffet, and lots of party games designed to get everyone on a first-name basis in a hurry. Tuesday through Thursday during the winter season, your **Evening on the Great River** starts with pick up at your hotel and a drive to the Montego River west of town; there you paddle upstream by torchlight in a dugout canoe, then hike a short distance to the "jungle clearing" where a recreated Awarak Indian village, drinks, dinner, and festive entertainment awaits. It all costs about $30 per person; make reservations through your hotel or call Great River Productions Ltd. (952–5047).

In Ocho Rios the same kind of fun happens on Sundays and is called **Jamaica Night on the White River.** In this case, the evening includes round-trip transportation from your hotel, a canoe ride up river, open bar, reggae-and-rock floor show, and dancing under the stars. One proviso: Remember to take mosquito repellent. Tickets cost about $25 for adults, $20 for children and should be purchased at your hotel activities desk. On Thursdays at 7:30 P.M. the **Dunn's River Feast** gets underway at the beach below the famed falls west of town. The lavish all-Jamaican buffet (roast suckling pig, for starters) and open bar are accompanied by reggae, dancers, a fashion show, goat races, and more. Admission is about $25 per adult, $20 per child.

THEATER, DANCE, AND CLASSICAL MUSIC

Jamaicans have an abiding fondness for the performing arts, and you can enjoy them, too, in the country's cultural center, Kingston. From late December through early spring, the **National Pantomime** performs its yearly update of *Trash* (from the local phrase "trash and ready," meaning "good"), a folk musical with original songs and dances, bright sets and costumes, and amusing commentary on current affairs. At the Ward Theater on North Parade. For info call 922–5988.

The concert season of the **Jamaica School of Dance** runs from late January to early February. Its interpretative dance based on Caribbean movements and themes is performed at the Little Theatre (926–6603), 4 Tom Redgam Avenue. The internationally known **National Dance Theatre Company** holds forth at the Little

Theatre for a few days in early December and then again for most of July. The NDTC Singers are also part of this group.

For classical music, check with your hotel activities desk or *The Daily Gleaner* for performances by the **Institute of Jamaica's School of Music,** the **Jamaica Philharmonic Symphony Orchestra,** and the **National Chorale.** Most concerts are in the early winter and early summer months.

SUNSETS BY WATER

If sunset-watching by land is *irie* ("excellent"), sunset-watching by sea is the *irie*-est. Strike up a friendship with a local yachtsman if you can. Failing that, there are a few seagoing outfits that will not only sail you into the sunset but ply you with grog and/or grub as well. These cruises last about two hours and cost $10 to $30.

In Montego Bay, two vessels that offer sunset cruises dock at On the Waterfront on Howard Cook Highway, opposite the Montego Bay Craft Market. You can be picked up at your hotel for either cruise. The **Calico** (952–5860), a 55-foot ketch, is an old wooden sailer kept in impeccable condition; it was used in the Walt Disney production, *Return to Treasure Island.* The **Topaz** (952–2955) is a 115-foot, square-rigged schooner.

From Port Antonio, the catamaran **Lady Jamaica** (no phone) makes a daily cocktail sail. Make arrangements through your hotel to climb aboard.

Shopping

Jamaica proves the adage that shoppers are made, not born. Not only is the potential for purchasing virtually limitless—from duty-free goods at substantial savings to island-made fashions, jewelry, wood carvings, straw work, and more—but the opportunity is *everywhere*.

Native entrepreneurs—known as higglers hereabouts—will approach you frequently and with varying degrees of persistence; they'll be trying to sell you everything from the illegal *ganja*—marijuana—to "gold" jewelry to a combination coin bank and ashtray fashioned from a length of bamboo. If you're not interested—and in the case of ganja, or any other illicit drug, to make a purchase is to risk arrest—say so firmly but politely; that will almost always suffice. If you are interested, it's negotiation time.

A rule of thumb about bargaining: If the item is marked with a price, chances are it is nonnegotiable.

DUTY-FREE SHOPPING

You *may* save as much as 40 to 50 percent off U.S.
prices. Then, again, you may save much less. A little
preplanning makes all the difference. Before you leave
home, decide what "in-bond" items you're interested
in—be they a Swiss timepiece, French perfume, British
woolens, Irish crystal, camera or recording gear, gold
jewelry, European crystal, porcelain, bone china, liquor
(including such Jamaican products as rums, the coffee
liqueur Tia Maria, or rum liqueur Rumona), tobacco products (Royal Jamaica cigars are prized), or Jamaican-
made fragrances like Khus Khus perfume or Royall
Lyme, Royall Spice, or Royall Bay after-shave for men.
Check U.S. prices. Then there will be no doubt.

Keep in mind, too, that you may still have to pay U.S.
Customs duty on any purchases that exceed the $400
limit per adult, which includes one liter of liquor.

Shopping duty-free goes like this: You must have
I.D. and pay with U.S. or Canadian currency, traveler's
check, or credit card. Liquor and tobacco products can
only be purchased at the airport or pier. Most in-bond
shops are grouped in shopping centers, in major hotels,
or at the airports. While the shops may have exclusive
brands or patterns, prices for types of merchandise are
about the same no matter where you go. Hours are standard, too—from 8:30 or 9 A.M. to 5 P.M. on weekdays, till
6 P.M. on Saturdays.

MADE IN JAMAICA

Jamaica is a country of crafts. Almost everyone, it
sometimes seems, is a fashioner of straw, wood, fabric,
beads, or gemstones. You can encounter amazing and
unexpected craftsmanship anywhere—at a rickety roadside stand, from a grinning local man who approaches

you on a street corner to a small boy who is an obvious expert at catching your eye and making his sales pitch.

Among the things Jamaicans do best: carvings, bowls, boxes, and other items made of lignum vitae, a rosy hardwood; woven straw baskets and mats; wicker furniture and other goods; beautiful hand-embroidered linens; cotton and silk batiked in stunning colors; stylish, silk-screened fashions; and jewelry made from black coral, coral agate, or shells.

Not everything you'll be asked to shell out for, of course, will be just the thing to remember your trip by, or the perfect gift for Aunt Lulu back home. Quality varies widely, and, as you might expect, most of the very best ends up in the tourist boutiques and shops at prices to match.

Our shopping strategy: If you find the *very* Jamaican-made thing you want, buy it then and there; except for, say, the most ordinary straw goods, it's not likely that you'll find that exact item elsewhere. (This is a land of individual artisans, not standardized tourist gimcracks.) But if you aren't quite sure, or think the price is too high, look for a reasonable facsimile—at a cheaper price—at one of the government-sponsored craft markets.

Now for the area-by-area rundown. . .

NEGRIL

The duty-free shop at **Hedonism II** (957–4326) on Norman Manley Boulevard at the northern end of the seven-mile beach has a modest selection of in-bond items.

Also browse the shops at Hedonism II (957–4200) for nicely crafted baskets and wood carvings, Jamaican-made resort wear, reggae recordings—and lots of T-shirts proclaiming the likes of "Ganja University."

You can test your bargaining prowess in the local market area near the Plaza de Negril and the office of the Jamaica Tourist Board. Beyond this the roadside stands, beach vendors, and local higglers rule the roost here.

MONTEGO BAY

At the airport, the **Montego Bay Duty Free Shop** (952–2377) handles electronic equipment and cameras by the likes of Nikon, Panasonic, and Vivitar. It's run by the same folks who have the **Chulani Camera Centre** (952–2158) in the City Centre Building near Sam Sharpe Square.

The **City Centre Building,** in fact, as well as the **Casa Montego Arcade** at the Casa Montego Hotel opposite Cornwall Beach have a cluster of duty-free shops. At the former, look for the **Presita Shop** (952–3261) for stereo and camera buys. At the latter, the MoBay branch of **Swiss Stores** (952–3087) carries an excellent selection of name-brand watches, electronic gear, and jewelry.

In the Rose Hall area, another **Swiss Stores** (953–2520) is at the Half Moon Club, as is the **Holiday Duty Free Shop** (953–2053), which specializes in photographic equipment. The Holiday Inn also houses a **Holiday Duty Free** (953–2503). And another mecca of duty-free shopping can be found at the **Holiday Village Shopping Centre** across Route A1 from the Holiday Inn.

For island-made crafts and foodstuffs, **Things Jamaican Ltd.** (952–1936) at the airport, has a small but interesting array. In the Montego Bay Freeport area, the **Tree Trunk Shop** (952–4911) has splendid offerings in Jamaican hardwood furnishings and wicker.

Along Harbour Street, near the wharves where fishermen unload their daily catch, is the **Crafts Market**. Bargain for the best deal on straw hats, baskets, mats, and other island products. For higher quality wood carvings and hand-turned bowls, look up the **Native Shop** (952–2992) at the Beachview Shopping Plaza on Gloucester Avenue.

For island fashions for women, **Ruth Clarage** has branches in Freeport (952–3278), in the Casa Montego Hotel (952–2282), and at Holiday Village (953–2579) across from the Holiday Inn in the Rose Hall area. Other fashionable options: the **Pineapple Shops** at Freeport

(952–0652) and the Montego Beach Hotel (952–5003) on Gloucester Avenue. **Elizabeth Jean** (952–3486), Beachview Arcade, has little nothings for the young and young at heart.

Among the best menswear retailers on the island is **Farel Ltd.** (952–3784) on Church Street near Sam Sharpe Square.

Blue Mountain Gems (953–2338) at Holiday Village creates its gorgeous jewelry on the premises, using black coral and other semiprecious stones.

FALMOUTH

At the Trelawny Beach Hotel east of town, this branch of **Chulani** specializes in savings on crystal (Waterford, Orrefors, and others), figurines (Hummel), and perfume.

Caribatik (954–3314), on the coast Route A1 two miles east of Falmouth, is worth a stop whether you're in the buying mood or not. This is the studio, shop, and gallery of Chicago-native Muriel Chandler, an engaging artist who has taken the vibrant colors of Jamaica and the surrounding sea, and has rendered them spectacularly onto baticked cotton and silk. As you would expect, you'll find batik shirts, ties, dresses, and caftans here, but you can also buy her fabric by the yard. Best of all, ask to see her gallery of batik "paintings"—many of which hang in homes, institutions, and collections the world over. Open mid-November to mid-May from 10 A.M. to 3 P.M., Tuesday through Saturday.

RUNAWAY BAY

Soni's (974–5104), in the lobby of the Runaway Bay Hotel, stocks Seiko and Pulsar watches, French perfumes, gold and ivory jewelry.

OCHO RIOS

Three duty-free shopping centers await to entice you. **Ocean Village,** the country's largest shopping plaza, is at seaside next to Turtle Beach Towers. **Swiss Stores** (974–2519) displays its Swiss watches, electronic equipment, and handcrafted jewelry there. **Soni's** (974–2303) has fine linens, French perfumes, gold chains, and ivory jewelry.

Pineapple Place is on the shoreside of Main Street in the heart of town. An impressive array of Japanese and German cameras and accessories are for sale at the **Caribbean Camera Centre** (974–2421). And **Casa De'O-ro** (974–2577) has jewelry, watches (Cartier, Corum, Gucci, Movado, Seiko, Swatch), and perfumes. A short walk east, on the inland side of the street opposite the Plantation Inn, is **Coconut Grove Shopping Centre.** Here, the many duty-free emporiums include **Americana Freeport Shop** (974–2414), which carries French perfumes, gold jewelry, linens, crystal (Waterford, Lalique, Swarovski), and china (Wedgwood, Royal Doulton).

For Jamaican-made gift items, sample **Living Wood** (974–2601), **The Craft Cottage** (974–2249), or **Under the Rainbow** (974–5158) in the Ocean Village Shopping Centre. The **Craft Park** in the heart of town is the place to make deals on straw goods, wood carvings, and the like.

Ruth Clarage has exclusive designs for both day and evening wear for women. Look for them at her stores in Pineapple Place (974–2658) and Ocean Village (974–2874). **Ting & Ting** (974–2968) stocks attractive, fun-in-the-sun clothes.

East of Ocho Rios on the coast road, **Harmony Hall** (974–4222) is a restored 19th-century great house devoted to the best in Jamaican contemporary art and artisans. One example among many: the distinctive and sought-after shell jewelry by Cindy Breakspeare, a former Miss World. It also has a gift shop with a good selection of books on Jamaica.

PORT ANTONIO

Sang Hing Giftland (993–2716) in the City Centre Plaza in the heart of town is the place to go for duty-free items. It stocks a treasure trove of imported bone china, crystal, figurines, jewelry, and more.

Craft hunting takes a little derring-do here. Follow your nose to the **Town Market** on West Street, where you'll strike your best deal and rub shoulders with the locals buying plantains and other staples. The hubbub is greatest on Thursdays and Saturdays. A more tranquil venue at which to pursue native hardwood furnishing and wicker is the shop aptly named **Oasis** (993–3745), 1 Harbour Street.

The widow of Hollywood legend Errol Flynn, Patricia Wymore Flynn, owns the small but charming boutique at Trident Villas and Hotel (993–2602) on the coast Route A4 east of town. And a branch of the excellent menswear retailer, **Farel Ltd.** (993–3311), is located at the City Centre Plaza.

KINGSTON

At the airport, you'll find branches of **Motta and Swiss Stores** (924–8023), which stock renowned watches (Juvenia, Omega, Patek Philippe, Piaget, Rolex, *et al.*), electronic gear (Sony, Panasonic, and many more), as well as one-of-a-kind jewelry. Other outlets are at the Jamaica Pegasus Hotel (929–8147) in New Kingston; 107 Harbour Street (922–8050); and the Constant Spring Mall (926–4861), 20 Constant Spring Road.

For Jamaican items you'll do no better than the shops behind Devon House that comprise **Things Jamaican Ltd.** (929–6602), 26 Hope Road. From a lignum-vitae coaster at under $1 to handmade four-poster beds at several hundred, this is a collection of the best craftsmanship on the island in a highly browsable, no-pressure setting. There's also a small shop at the airport (924–8556).

Near the cruise piers on the harbor, the **Jamaica Crafts Market** (922–3015), 52 Port Royal Street, houses a vast assortment of handmade items, with a special bounty of straw and woven goods and wood carvings. Hours are 8 A.M. to 5 P.M. Monday to Friday; open till 6 P.M. Saturdays.

Kingston has a number of shopping centers and plazas. The **Constant Spring Mall,** 20 Constant Spring Road, is one of the largest. But the chic-est and most civilized is certainly the **New Kingston Shopping Centre** on Dominica Drive across from the Tourism Centre Building. On two levels, with an open-air central court that has a gurgling fountain and reflecting pool, it also boasts free underground parking and a food court. Check out the gleaming hardwood furnishings at **Skandia** (929–8630), the stylish sportswear and swim-wear at **Just Wright** (929–8612), and the fashions for women at **California by Philip** (929–4373). Among the three dozen shops, boutiques, and restaurants is even an extremely fancy **Woolworth's** (929–8632).

Nearby, at the Wyndham New Kingston Hotel (926–5430) is a branch of **Ruth Clarage,** a name to remember for well-made day and evening wear in colorful but classy island designs. In an art- or book-buying mood? Head for **Bolivar Bookshop and Gallery** (926–8799) at Grove and Half Way Tree roads.

MANDEVILLE

Mandeville has four shopping plazas. **Willogate Shopping Centre** is at Wesley and Manchester roads. **Grove Court Shopping Centre** is just off the town square. **Caledonia Shopping Centre** is on Caledonia Road near South Race Course.

Manchester Shopping Centre is also on Caledonia Road, near Newgreen Road. For island-made souvenirs here, check out **Craft Things Jamaican** (962–3363).

The **SWA Craft Centre** (962–1676) on Caledonia Road provides employment for girls who dropped out of school but cannot find regular jobs. Here they do embroidery, crochet work and make pastry, cakes, toys, and clothing.

Index

Index

FODOR'S TRAVEL GUIDES

Here is a complete list of Fodor's Travel Guides, available in current editions; most are also available in a British edition published by Hodder & Stoughton.

U.S. GUIDES

Alaska
American Cities (Great Travel Values)
Arizona including the Grand Canyon
Atlantic City & the New Jersey Shore
Boston
California
Cape Cod & the Islands of Martha's Vineyard & Nantucket
Carolinas & the Georgia Coast
Chesapeake
Chicago
Colorado
Dallas/Fort Worth
Disney World & the Orlando Area (Fun in)
Far West
Florida
Forth Worth (see Dallas)
Galveston (see Houston)
Georgia (see Carolinas)
Grand Canyon (see Arizona)
Greater Miami & the Gold Coast
Hawaii
Hawaii (Great Travel Values)
Houston & Galveston
I-10: California to Florida
I-55: Chicago to New Orleans
I-75: Michigan to Florida
I-80: San Francisco to New York
I-95: Maine to Miami
Jamestown (see Williamsburg)
Las Vegas including Reno & Lake Tahoe (Fun in)
Los Angeles & Nearby Attractions
Martha's Vineyard (see Cape Cod)
Maui (Fun in)
Nantucket (see Cape Cod)
New England
New Jersey (see Atlantic City)
New Mexico
New Orleans
New Orleans (Fun in)
New York City
New York City (Fun in)
New York State
Orlando (see Disney World)
Pacific North Coast
Philadelphia
Reno (see Las Vegas)
Rockies
San Diego & Nearby Attractions
San Francisco (Fun in)
San Francisco plus Marin County & the Wine Country
The South
Texas
U.S.A.
Virgin Islands (U.S. & British)

Virginia
Waikiki (Fun in)
Washington, D.C.
Williamsburg, Jamestown & Yorktown

FOREIGN GUIDES

Acapulco (see Mexico City)
Acapulco (Fun in)
Amsterdam
Australia, New Zealand & the South Pacific
Austria
The Bahamas
The Bahamas (Fun in)
Barbados (Fun in)
Beijing, Guangzhou & Shanghai
Belgium & Luxembourg
Bermuda
Brazil
Britain (Great Travel Values)
Canada
Canada (Great Travel Values)
Canada's Maritime Provinces plus Newfoundland & Labrador
Cancún, Cozumel, Mérida & the Yucatán
Caribbean
Caribbean (Great Travel Values)
Central America
Copenhagen (see Stockholm)
Cozumel (see Cancún)
Eastern Europe
Egypt
Europe
Europe (Budget)
France
France (Great Travel Values)
Germany: East & West
Germany (Great Travel Values)
Great Britain
Greece
Guangzhou (see Beijing)
Helsinki (see Stockholm)
Holland
Hong Kong & Macau
Hungary
India, Nepal & Sri Lanka
Ireland
Israel
Italy
Italy (Great Travel Values)
Jamaica (Fun in)
Japan
Japan (Great Travel Values)
Jordan & the Holy Land
Kenya
Korea
Labrador (see Canada's Maritime Provinces)
Lisbon
Loire Valley
London

London (Fun in)
London (Great Travel Values)
Luxembourg (see Belgium)
Macau (see Hong Kong)
Madrid
Mazatlan (see Mexico's Baja)
Mexico
Mexico (Great Travel Values)
Mexico City & Acapulco
Mexico's Baja & Puerto Vallarta, Mazatlan, Manzanillo, Copper Canyon
Montreal (Fun in)
Munich
Nepal (see India)
New Zealand
Newfoundland (see Canada's Maritime Provinces)
1936 . . . on the Continent
North Africa
Oslo (see Stockholm)
Paris
Paris (Fun in)
People's Republic of China
Portugal
Province of Quebec
Puerto Vallarta (see Mexico's Baja)
Reykjavik (see Stockholm)
Rio (Fun in)
The Riviera (Fun on)
Rome
St. Martin/St. Maarten (Fun in)
Scandinavia
Scotland
Shanghai (see Beijing)
Singapore
South America
South Pacific
Southeast Asia
Soviet Union
Spain
Spain (Great Travel Values)
Sri Lanka (see India)
Stockholm, Copenhagen, Oslo, Helsinki & Reykjavik
Sweden
Switzerland
Sydney
Tokyo
Toronto
Turkey
Vienna
Yucatán (see Cancún)
Yugoslavia

SPECIAL-INTEREST GUIDES

Bed & Breakfast Guide: North America
Royalty Watching
Selected Hotels of Europe
Selected Resorts and Hotels of the U.S.
Ski Resorts of North America
Views to Dine by around the World

AVAILABLE AT YOUR LOCAL BOOKSTORE OR WRITE TO FODOR'S TRAVEL
PUBLICATIONS, INC., 201 EAST 50th STREET, NEW YORK, NY 10022.